DAS
TRAININGS-
BUCH

W0299944

Englisch Grammatik 5–7

In 3 Schritten zum Lernerfolg!

Schroedel

DAS TRAININGS-BUCH

Englisch Grammatik 5–7

Autorin:

Lara Jost unterrichtet Englisch an einer Gesamtschule von der Unter- bis zur Oberstufe. Englisch ist neben Deutsch ihre zweite Muttersprache. Neben ihrer Unterrichtstätigkeit verfügt sie über langjährige Erfahrung als Nachhilfelehrerin. Sie ist Verfasserin von Lernhilfen und von Publikationen zum Thema Theaterspiel im Fremdsprachenunterricht.

Druck [2] / Jahr 2016

Redaktion: imprint, Zusmarshausen
Kontakt: lernhilfen@schroedel.de
Layout: Druckreif! Sandra Grünberg, Braunschweig
Umschlaggestaltung: Janssen Kahlert Design und Kommunikation GmbH, Hannover
Umschlagfoto: Frîa Hagen
Illustrationen: Thies Schwarz, Hannover
Satz: imprint, Zusmarshausen
Druck und Bindung: Westermann Druck Zwickau GmbH

ISBN 978-3-507-**23224**-2

Liebe Schülerin, lieber Schüler,

du willst sicherer in der englischen Grammatik werden?
Dann ist das Trainingsbuch genau das Richtige für dich! Mithilfe der 3-Schritt-Methode kannst du hier alle Regeln üben, die in der 5.–7. Klasse wichtig sind.

Die 3-Schritt-Methode ist ganz einfach.

1 Verstehen: Lies die **Grammatikregel** gründlich durch und merke dir den Inhalt.

2 Üben: Abwechslungsreiche **Übungen** helfen, die Grammatikregel zu verinnerlichen.

3 Können: Schließlich schreibst du einen **Test**, um zu überprüfen, ob du die Regel wirklich verstanden hast.

Die Lösungen für die Übungen und Tests findest du ab Seite 158. Hier findest du auch die Auswertungen zu den einzelnen Tests.

Und jetzt kann es auch schon losgehen.

Viel Erfolg beim Üben mit dem Trainingsbuch!
Lara Jost

Inhalt

1. Verben

1.1 Regelmäßige und unregelmäßige Verben

5. Schuljahr Regelmäßige Verben ... 6
5. Schuljahr Unregelmäßige Verben ... 10

1.2 Die Hilfsverben

5. Schuljahr be, have, do ... 14

1.3 Die Zeiten

5. Schuljahr Gegenwart – simple present und present progressive ... 20
5. Schuljahr Die einfache Vergangenheit – simple past ... 26
6. Schuljahr Die Zeit »dazwischen« – present perfect ... 32
7. Schuljahr Die »Sherlock-Holmes-Zeit« – past progressive ... 36
7. Schuljahr Die Zeiten der Zukunft – will-future and going-to-future ... 42
7. Schuljahr Die Vorvergangenheit – past perfect ... 46

1.4 Modalverben

5. Schuljahr can, can't, must, mustn't, need, needn't ... 50
5. Schuljahr have to, be allowed to, be able to ... 54
7. Schuljahr may/might/should/ought to ... 58

1.5 Gerund

6. Schuljahr Gerund als Subjekt oder Objekt ... 60
7. Schuljahr Gerund nach Präpositionen ... 62

2. Präpositionen

5. Schuljahr Zeitangaben: Tagesdatum, Monate und Jahre ... 64
6. Schuljahr Zeitangaben und Ortsangaben ... 66
7. Schuljahr Ortsangaben und Richtungsangaben ... 68

3. Nomen

5. Schuljahr Groß- und Kleinschreibung ... 70
5. Schuljahr Pluralformen ... 72
7. Schuljahr Pluralformen: one, ones ... 76
5. Schuljahr Genitiv: Possessive 's ... 78
6. Schuljahr Possessive Plural, 's-Genitiv oder of-Genitiv ... 80
7. Schuljahr Besonderheiten des 's-Genitiv und Ortsangaben mit 's-Genitiv ... 84
5. Schuljahr much, many/a lot of/some, any ... 86
6. Schuljahr some, any, no – Zusammensetzungen mit some und any ... 88
7. Schuljahr Zählbare und nicht zählbare Nomen ... 90

4. Pronomen

Personalpronomen und Possessivbegleiter .... 92 — 5. Schuljahr
Possessivpronomen .... 96 — 6. Schuljahr
Reflexivpronomen und each other .... 98 — 7. Schuljahr

5. Artikel

Der unbestimmte Artikel a, an – der bestimmte Artikel the .... 102 — 5. Schuljahr

6. Adjektive und Adverbien

Adjektiv oder Adverb? .... 106 — 5. Schuljahr
Steigerung der Adjektive .... 112 — 6. Schuljahr
Vergleiche mit Adjektiven as … as, … than … .... 116 — 7. Schuljahr

7. Adverbien

Häufigkeitsadverbien und Stellung im Satz .... 120 — 6. Schuljahr
Adverbiale Bestimmung und Stellung im Satz .... 124 — 7. Schuljahr

8. Satzbau

Aussagesatz, Imperativ, Fragesatz .... 128 — 5. Schuljahr

9. If-Sätze

If-Satz Typ 1: Wahrscheinlichkeit .... 132 — 6. Schuljahr
If-Satz Typ 2 und Typ 3: unwahrscheinlich und unmöglich .... 136 — 7. Schuljahr

10. Relativsätze

Relativsätze mit und ohne Relativpronomen .... 140 — 6. Schuljahr
Freie Relativsätze .... 146 — 7. Schuljahr

11. Konjunktionen

Bindewörter: and, but, or, so, because .... 148 — 5. Schuljahr
Konjunktionen: because, because of, when .... 150 — 6. Schuljahr
Konjunktionen Zeit, Bedingung, Gegensatz, Ursache .... 154 — 7. Schuljahr

Lösungen 158

Glossar 202

Stichwortverzeichnis 206

1. Verben

1.1 Regelmäßige und unregelmäßige Verben

1

Regelmäßige Verben

Im Englischen gibt es zwei Verbformen, die regelmäßigen Verben und die unregelmäßigen Verben, die du brauchst, um die verschiedenen Zeiten, zum Beispiel die einfache Gegenwart (simple present), zu bilden.

Bei regelmäßigen Verben brauchst du nur die Grundform (infinitive), um alle Formen abzuleiten. Es wird einfach ein -ed an die Grundform angehängt.

I work at home – I worked at home – I have worked ...

1. Form	2. Form	3. Form
infinitive	**simple past**	**past participle**
(to) play	played	played
(to) kiss	kissed	kissed

Tipp:
-**y** am Verbende wird zu -**ied**.
carry → carried
Ausnahmen sind play und stay.
played, stayed
Wenn die letzten drei Buchstaben Konsonant/Vokal/Konsonant sind, verdoppeln sich **b, d, m, p, s und t**.
stop → stopped
Endet ein Verb auf einem **stummen e**, so entfällt dieses bei der Anfügung von **-ed. phone → phoned**

2

1. *Bilde von diesen regelmäßigen Verben die 2. und die 3. Form.*

a) (to) listen ....

b) (to) work ....

c) (to) look ....

d) (to) stop ....

e) (to) want ....

f) (to) use ....

2. *Finde die fünf Verben mit -ed-Endung in der Wortschlange.*

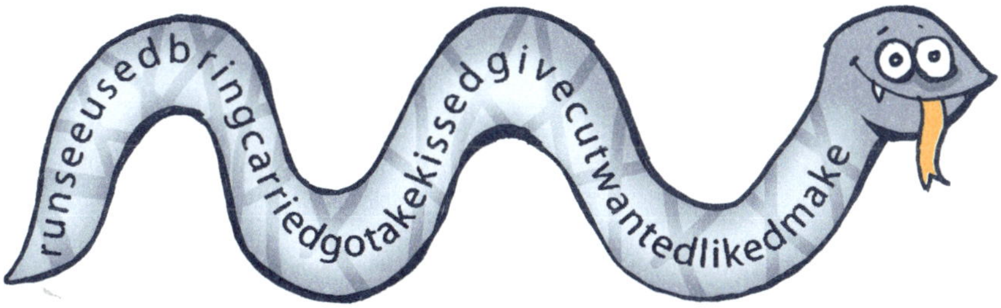

a) .... b) .... c) ....

d) .... e) ....

3. *Schreibe die fünf Verben aus Aufgabe 2 in der Grundform.*

a) .... b) .... c) ....

d) .... e) ....

4. *Die Sätze sollten in der 2. Form stehen. Finde die Fehler und korrigiere den ganzen Satz.*

a) My brother playd tennis yesterday.

....

b) My sister listen to music.

....

c) My father cookeed lunch.

....

Verben

d) My mother watches TV.

....

e) My dog wantet to eat.

....

f) I loveed my family.

....

5. *Male die regelmäßigen Verben blau und die unregelmäßigen Verben orange an.*

go come want play see take live run
laugh sing drink eat buy sell cry
shout become be love

6. *Nimm alle regelmäßigen Verben aus Aufgabe 5 und bilde mit ihnen in deinem Heft alle drei Formen.*

7. *Vervollständige die Sätze mit einem passenden Verb aus Aufgabe 5.*

a) I .... tennis.

b) I .... when I see funny films.

c) I .... an ice cream, please.

d) I .... my family.

e) I .... in London.

f) I always .... when my grandmother goes away.

g) I don't want to .... at my brother.

Test

3

1. *Finde die regelmäßigen Verben in diesem Wortsalat.*

S	S	E	Y	I	S	C	O	F	O	L
S	E	E	N	S	A	W	B	C	M	O
L	L	I	S	T	E	N	X	U	G	O
I	O	P	L	A	Y	E	R	K	A	K
V	R	E	C	L	U	E	V	I	D	A
E	W	O	R	K	X	D	I	S	N	X
B	O	L	A	E	B	Y	D	S	E	F
U	S	O	T	D	H	Q	E	Q	V	I
D	T	H	E	O	S	P	O	B	T	H

a) .... b) .... c) .... d) ....

e) .... f) .... g) .... h) ....

2. *Vervollständige die Tabelle, indem du die fehlenden Formen einsetzt.*

a) .... worked

b) .... loved ....

c) (to) carry ....

d) .... wanted

e) .... looked ....

f) (to) phone ....

Verben

1

Unregelmäßige Verben

Wie du weißt, gibt es im Englischen zwei Verbformen, die regelmäßigen Verben und die unregelmäßigen Verben, die du brauchst, um die verschiedenen Zeiten, zum Beispiel die einfache Gegenwart (simple present), zu bilden.

Bei den unregelmäßigen Verben musst du alle drei Verbformen auswendig lernen, da sich die 2. und 3. Form nicht ableiten lassen. Im Folgenden findest du **einige wichtige** unregelmäßige Verben.

Ausführliche Listen findest du in deinem Schulbuch.

1.Form	2. Form	3. Form
infinitive	**simple past**	**past participle**
(to) be	was/were	been
(to) begin	began	begun
(to) bring	brought	brought
(to) buy	bought	bought
(to) catch	caught	caught
(to) choose	chose	chosen
(to) come	came	come
(to) cost	cost	cost
(to) cut	cut	cut
(to) do	did	done
(to) drink	drank	drunk
(to) drive	drove	driven
(to) eat	ate	eaten
(to) fall	fell	fallen
(to) feel	felt	felt
(to) fly	flew	flown
(to) forget	forgot	forgotten
(to) get	got	got
(to) give	gave	given
(to) go	went	gone
(to) have	had	had
(to) hear	heard	heard
(to) keep	kept	kept
(to) know	knew	known
(to) leave	left	left
(to) lend	lent	lent
(to) lose	lost	lost
(to) make	made	made

(to) see	saw	seen
(to) throw	threw	thrown
(to) give	gave	given
(to) meet	met	met
(to) read	read	read
(to) take	took	taken

2

1. *Hier haben sich Fehler eingeschlichen. Findest du sie? Markiere sie. Du kannst die Tabelle auf dieser Doppelseite zuhilfe nehmen.*

(to) be	was/were	be
(to) buy	buyed	bought
(to) came	come	come
(to) drink	drink	drinked

2. *Ergänze die fehlenden Formen.*

a)	become	....	....
b)	....	brought	....
c)	drink	....	....
d)	....	....	felt
e)	....	heard	....
f)	lose	....	....

3. *Markiere regelmäßige Verben mit einem ■ und unregelmäßige Verben mit einem ▲.*

feel	work	listen
make	become	look

Verben

4. *Lies den Text und korrigiere die falschen Verbformen.*

London is a fascinating city. It is the capitol of the United Kingdom and lies on the river Thames. Many famous people of the past been Londoners. For example Michael Faraday who "invent" electricity, or John Keats who writes famous poems. These people be born in the late 18th century. Charlie Chaplin make films which still make us laugh today and Alfred Hitchcock directes movies that still scare us and both men were Londoners, too. Daniel Day Lewis, who has act in several Hollywood movies and David Beckham, the famous football star be also Londoners.

1 .... 2 ....

3 .... 4 ....

5 .... 6 ....

7 .... 8 ....

5. *Was für ein Durcheinander! Versuche die Formen in der Tabelle unten richtig einzusortieren.*

made see make felt

felt feel saw seen made

....

....

....

Test

1. *Vervollständige die Tabelle.*

a) forget	....	....
b)	gave	....
c) drink	....	....
d)	....	known
e)	began	....
f) fly	....	....

2. *Lies den Text und setze das Verb jeweils in der 2. Form ein. Es handelt sich nicht immer um regelmäßige Verben.*

Dear Liza,

We are now in Spain. Finally my summer holidays can begin. We .... (arrive) late at night and it .... (be) dark. We .... (look) for our hotel but all the names .... (be) in Spanish, so we .... (stop) and .... (ask) an old man for directions. He .... (speak) to us in Spanish, so we .... (have) to guess what he .... (mean). Then my father .... (see) a big sign with the name of our hotel. This morning I .... (wake) up to the sound of the waves and the seagulls.

Holidays – here I come!

Yours Melinda

1.2 Die Hilfsverben

1

be, have, do

Be, have und do können sowohl Hilfsverben als auch Vollverben sein.

Als Vollverb bedeutet be **sein**.

I am a rockstar. Ich bin ein Rockstar.

Als Hilfsverb benötigst du das Verb **be**, um die progressiven Zeitformen und das Passiv zu bilden.

I am (I'm)	I'm not	I was	I wasn't
you are (you're)	you aren't	you were	you weren't
he/she/it is (he's)	he isn't	he was	he wasn't
we are (we're)	we aren't	we were	we weren't
you are (you're)	you aren't	you were	you weren't
they are (they're)	they aren't	they were	they weren't

Du kannst das Verb have als Vollverb benutzen.

I had a headache. Ich hatte Kopfschmerzen.

Im Präsens benutzt man – vor allem im britischen Englisch – die Form **have got**. In der Verneinung fällt das **got** weg.

I have got a dog. I don't have a dog.

Als Hilfsverb benötigt man das Verb have, um die Perfektformen zu bilden.

It has been a fantastic concert. I had been a teacher for quite a few years.

I have (I've)	I haven't	I had	I hadn't
you have (you've)	you haven't	you had	you hadn't
he/she/it has (he's)	he hasn't	he had	he hadn't
we have (we've)	we haven't	we had	we hadn't
you have (you've)	you haven't	you had	you hadn't
they have (they've)	they haven't	they had	they hadn't

Das Verb do kannst du als Vollverb benutzen.

Mother often does the washing in the morning. I often do my homework in the afternoon.

Wenn do das Vollverb in deinem Satz ist, brauchst du für Fragen und Verneinungen zusätzlich do/did als Hilfsverb.

I do my homework. Do I do my homework? I don't do my homework.

Als Hilfsverb benötigst du do, um bei allen Vollverben die Fragen, die Verneinungen und die verneinte Befehlsform zu bilden.

Do you go to school? I don't go to school. Don't go to school.

I do	I don't	I did	I didn't
you do	you don't	you did	you didn't
he/she/it does	he doesn't	he did	he didn't
we do	we don't	we did	we didn't
you do	you don't	you did	you didn't
they do	they don't	they did	they didn't

Tipp:
Mit dem Wort **there** und einer Form von **be**, kannst du ausdrücken, dass etwas vorhanden ist (There is one boy in the room.), etwas existiert (There are elephants in India.) oder etwas passiert ist (There was a bad storm last night.).

1. *there is oder there are?*

2

a) .... a new girl in our class.

b) .... some crayons in the cupboard.

c) .... a lot of noise!

d) .... a spider in my bag.

2. *Setze die Sätze aus Aufgabe 1 in die Vergangenheit:* ***there was*** *oder* ***there were****.*

a) ....

b) ....

c) ....

d) ....

Verben

3. *Setze **has (got)** oder **have (got)** ein.*

Mum: What is wrong Lena?

Lena: I can't find my ipod. Where is it?

Mum: .... your brother .... your ipod in his bed?

Lena: No, he .... Very strange, Mum.

Mum: I really don't know. .... Laura and Ella ....
an ipod, too?

Lena: No, they .... They .... an old CD-player.
Hm. Maybe they .... my ipod?

Mum: Let's look in their room. – Yes, they .... it!

4. *Setze **do**, **does** oder **did** ein.*

a) .... you often get together with your friends on the weekends?

b) Ivy .... her homework every day.

c) .... the teacher forget her book again yesterday?

d) .... your mother go to work every day?

e) He always .... the dishes.

f) How many paper planes .... you build every day?

Tipp:
Um eine Frage mit **Fragewort (where, why, when, how, who)** und einer Form von **be**, **do** oder **have** zu stellen, musst du das Fragewort an den Anfang des Satzes stellen.

Why did she scream? Where have you been? What does he know?

5. *Bilde die Frage, indem du ein passendes Fragewort mit der richtigen Form von **do** oder **have** verwendest.*

a) .... you want to do tomorrow?

b) .... she always scream like that?

c) .... you been?

d) .... much .... these earrings cost?

e) .... he got in that bag?

f) .... I look like this?

g) .... they arrive home?

6. *Hier haben sich ein paar Fehler eingeschlichen. Findest Du sie?*

a) I has got a pony.

b) Do you have got a pony, too?

c) What has you done?

d) How do he know about it?

e) Does you like ice-cream?

f) Who have got the tickets?

7. *Lies den Text und setze die Bausteine an die richtige Stelle.*

has | there was | there was | does | have | did | there were | there is | do

Dear Diary,

.... something I must tell you! I .... not .... a lot of time, but I will try to tell you quickly. Last week .... a flea market in town. Remember, that I saw

Verben

this beautiful red bike at my friend's house some time ago? Well, ... many people at the market and they had many different things to sell. Suddenly Daddy said: "........................ you see that red bike?" Of course I saw it! And guess what? I .... got a red bike now. My friend .... got a green bike. Sometimes .... some really nice things at flea markets!

3

Test

1. *Lies die Antworten und schreibe die Fragen dazu auf. Verwende das entsprechende Fragewort, falls nötig, und die richtige Form von „do“ oder „have“.*

a) ....? Yes, I like animals.

b) ....? No, she doesn't have a pony.

c) ....? I do my homework in the afternoon.

d) ....? She screamed because she saw a spider.

e) ....? Benjamin has got the tickets.

f) ....? I just went out to buy some milk.

2. *Finde den Fehler.*
Schreibe die Sätze korrigiert in dein Heft.

a) There are a flea market in town!
b) There is many things to see at a flea market.
c) There is no bikes under that Christmas tree!
d) There was a lot of bikes at her friend's house.
e) There were a lovely red bike at the flea market.
f) There are always a surprise waiting for you!

3. *Sage auf Englisch, dass …*
Schreibe in dein Heft.

a) du jeden Tag deine Hausaufgaben machst.
b) dein Freund einen neuen Hund hat.
c) viele Menschen auf dem Flohmarkt waren.

4. *Frage auf Englisch, dass …*
Schreibe in dein Heft.
a) ob sie in London wohnt.
b) was sie weiß.
c) warum er immer so schreit.

5. *Verbinde die Satzteile sinnvoll miteinander.*

When did	you been?
There is	we do about this?
Who has got	many people at a flea market?
What do	a lot of homework today.
Where have	you find out?
Are there	an idea?

1.3 Die Zeiten

1

Gegenwart – simple present und present progressive

Es gibt zwei Zeitformen, das simple present und das present progressive, mit denen du etwas in der Gegenwart ausdrücken kannst.

Wann werden simple present und present progressive verwendet? Du verwendest das simple present, um zu betonen, dass jemand etwas regelmäßig oder gewohnheitsmäßig tut.

Ben goes to school every morning.

Oder, um zu sagen, dass etwas immer gleich ist.

Ben speaks German and English.

Present progressive verwendest du, um auszudrücken, was jemand in diesem Moment macht.

Ben is doing his homework at the moment.

Wie werden simple present und present progressive gebildet?

Zeit	Aussagesatz	Frage	Verneinung
simple present	Grundform he, she, it: + -s **I play, she plays**	do + Grundform does + Grundform (he, she, it) **Do I sing?** **Does she go?**	don't + Grundform doesn't + Grundform **I don't know.** **She doesn't sing.**
present progres-sive	am/is/are + Verb + -ing **I am playing.** **She is singing.** **We are giving.**	am/is/are zuerst, Verb + -ing **Am I playing?** **Is she singing?** **Are we giving?**	am/is/are + not **I am not playing.** **She is not singing.** **We are not giving.**

Tipp:
Einige Verben drücken keine Aktivität aus, sondern beschreiben Zustände. Diese werden normalerweise nur im simple present verwendet.

be, believe, hate, hear, know, like, love, need, see, understand, want.

1. *Entscheide, wann du simple present und wann du present progressive verwenden musst.*

2

	simple present	present progressive
a) Ich spiele jeden Mittwoch Fußball.	☐	☐
b) Ich telefoniere gerade mit meiner Freundin.	☐	☐
c) Tom geht oft mit seinem Hund zum See.	☐	☐
d) Schau mal! Ein Doppeldeckerbus!	☐	☐
e) Wir fliegen jedes Jahr nach Spanien!	☐	☐
f) Schläfst du schon?	☐	☐

Tipp:
Endet das Verb auf -**s** oder einen Zischlaut musst du -**es** anhängen (he watch**es**).
Endet das Verb auf Konsonant + y (try): -y mit s wird zu -**ies** (she tr**ies**).
Y nach Vokal: -**s** anhängen (she play**s**).
Aus go und do wird go**es** und do**es**, aus dem Verb to have wird ha**s**.

2. *Schreibe die Verben in der richtigen Form (Grundform oder mit -s).*

Hello, my name is Anne. I .... (speak) German and English. My parents are from Germany, but we ....

(live) in London. My brother, Tim, is six years old and he ....
(love) London. He .... (think) it is very exciting. His favorite place is London Zoo. I .... (like) London but I .... (miss) my old home in Germany. We often .... (go) to visit our grandmother Elisabeth.

3. *Ergänze die Sätze mithilfe der Bilder.*

a) Ben likes carrots, but he

....

b) I play tennis, but I

....

c) We live in England, we

....

d) Tim has got a dog, he

....

4. *Sag auf Englisch, dass …*

a) du in Deutschland lebst. ....

....

b) dein Freund Bananen nicht mag. ....

....

c) dein kleiner Bruder sechs Jahre alt ist. ....

....

5. *Frage auf Englisch, ob …*

a) der Vater deines Freundes Englisch und Deutsch spricht. ....

....

b) deine Freunde Pizza wollen. ....

....

c) Chantal Französisch spricht. ....

....

6. *Finde den Fehler und korrigiere!*

a) At the moment I am stand in the rain. ....

....

b) Benjamin play basketball every Thursday. ....

....

c) Mum and Dad playing tennis now. ....

....

d) I never eats salad! ....

....

e) Doing you like chocolate? ....

....

Tipp:
Present progressive: Endet das Verb auf -e, dann entfällt dieses bei der Bildung des progressive (**give → I am giving**). -ie am Ende des Verbs wird zu -y: **lie → She is lying**.
Sind die letzten drei Buchstaben Konsonant/Vokal/Konsonant, wird der letzte Buchstabe verdoppelt: **stop → We are stopping**.

Verben

7. *Verneine die folgenden Sätze.*

a) I am sleeping. ....

b) My family likes football. ....

....

c) You go to London Zoo every day. ....

....

d) My mother is talking to a friend. ....

....

e) Kate and Samira collect everything about horses. ....

....

f) The dog is looking at you. ....

....

8. *Finde die Frage zur Antwort.*

a) .... a cup of tea?

No, it isn't. The gorilla ....

....

b) ....?

No, it isn't. The bird ....

....

c) ....?

No, it isn't. The dog ....

....

Test

3

1. *Sage auf Englisch, dass …*

a) du jeden Tag deiner Mutter hilfst. ....

....

b) deine Schwester jetzt gerade zu Mittag isst. ....

....

2. *Frage auf Englisch, ob …*

a) deine Mutter jetzt schon schläft. ....

....

b) Sarah jeden Tag fern sieht. ....

....

3. *Finde die richtige Frage.*

a) ....?

Yes, she is talking to her friend. (Mum / talk / friend)

b) ....?

No, the bear loves honey. (bear / love/salad)

4. *Vervollständige die Sätze mithilfe der richtigen Verneinung.*

a) Luka eats apples, but he .... (eat) bananas.

b) Anna is reading a book, she .... (write) a book.

Verben

1

Die einfache Vergangenheit – simple past

Die einfache Vergangenheit, das simple past, verwendest du, wenn eine Handlung abgeschlossen ist (in anderen Worten: Wenn etwas aus und vorbei ist). Typische Signalwörter stehen meist am Ende oder ganz am Anfang des Satzes.

yesterday, last week, last month, last year,
10/20/100 years + ago

Jahreszahlen aus der Vergangenheit, zum Beispiel 1975, können auch ein Hinweis sein.

Wie wird das simple past verwendet?

Zeit	Aussagesatz	Frage	Verneinung
simple past	Regelmäßige Verben: Grundform + -ed **I played, she played** Unregelmäßige Verben: 2. Form **I began, she wrote**	did + Grundform **Did you sing?** Außer bei was/were: **Was Ben at home? Were they blind?**	didn't + grundform **I didn't know. She didn't sing. Außer bei was/were: She wasn't sad. They weren't at home.**

Tipp:
Folgende Wörter solltest du dir merken:
can → could; have → has, had; am/is → was; are → were.

2

1. *Finde die Fehler. Markiere sie farbig.*

a) Yesterday I go to see my best friend.
b) There we meets some friends and a dog.
c) We all playing football.
d) We had to stop because the dog ated the ball.

2. *Setze die Sätze ins simple past!*

a) Benjamin has a dog. ....

....

b) We live in London. ....

....

c) My parents don't go to New York. ....

....

d) I write a letter to my grandmother. ....

....

3. *Sage auf Englisch, dass …*

a) du gestern in der Schule warst. ....

....

b) Layla letzte Woche nicht in die Schule gegangen ist. ....

....

c) der Lehrer krank (ill) war. ....

....

4. *Frage auf Englisch, ob …*

a) Timmy gestern in der Schule war. ....

....

b) ich meine Hausaufgaben gestern gemacht habe. ....

....

c) Mike das Mittagessen mochte. ....

....

Tipp:
-y am Verbende wird zu **-ied** (carry → carr**ied**).
Ausnahmen sind play und stay (played, stayed)
Wenn die letzten drei Buchstaben Konsonant/Vokal/Konsonant sind, verdoppeln sich **b, d, m, p, s** und **t** (stop → sto**pp**ed). Endet ein Verb auf einem **stummen e**, fällt dieses weg (phone → phoned).

Verben

5. *Chip, das kleine Gespenst erzählt von seinem früheren Leben. Markiere die Fehler, die sich eingeschlichen haben, und schreibe den Text neu und ohne Fehler in dein Heft.*

300 years ago I liveed in a big castle in Ireland. My parents was wise and had a good heart. I do not have brothers or sisters. I plaied on my own most of the time. But one day something terrible happens.
There was a big fire and I am the only one who die. Because I miss my family so much, I still live in the castle today.

6. *Entscheide ob simple present, present progressive oder simple past eingesetzt werden müssen.
Die Signalwörter helfen dir dabei.*

Anna and her family .... (go) to Scotland every year. At the moment they .... (visit) a friend, Mr McVarady who .... (live) in an old castle. At the moment Anne .... (talk) to Mr McVaraday. Anna: "Mr McVarady, ... you .... (live) here alone?"
"Yes, Anne", says Mr McVarady. "I live here alone. Well, not really, because there is Bernadette. She is the White Lady. She .... (be) a ghost. She .... (live) here 300 years ago and had a sad life. But you .... (not/have) to be afraid. She is a friendly ghost."
Anna .... (not/like) ghosts. Yesterday she .... (see) a lady in the garden! She .... (run) away at once!

7. *Ordne die Signalwörter den Sätzen zu.*

a) I visit my best friend in Ireland …	1) 300 years ago.
b) Anna is telling her best friend about her holiday …	2) often.
c) I dream of castles and ghosts …	3) sometimes.
d) Chip lived in a castle …	4) at the moment.
e) Guests can see the White Lady …	5) every year.
f) The White Lady did not show herself …	6) last month.

a + 5 ……………………………………………………………………………………

8. *Finde die passende Frage zur vorgegebenen Antwort.*

a) ……………………………………………………………………………………

Yes, yesterday I watched a movie.

b) ……………………………………………………………………………………

Ben came home at 8 o'clock yesterday.

c) ……………………………………………………………………………………

No, we weren't at home. We went out yesterday evening.

d) ……………………………………………………………………………………

No, we didn't meet Sally at the cinema.

9. *Richtig oder falsch? Kreuze an.*

	R	F
a) He carryd her home.	☐	☐
b) Yesterday we went to the cinema.	☐	☐
c) Chip lives many years ago.	☐	☐

Verben

3 Test

1. *Sage auf Englisch, dass …*

a) Chip vor 300 Jahren lebte. ....

....

b) Chips Eltern nette Leute waren. ....

....

c) Chip keine Hunde mochte. ....

....

d) Anna eine Frau im Garten sah. ....

....

e) Mr McVarady die weiße Dame traf. ....

....

f) Anna mit der weißen Dame sprach. ....

....

2. *Schau dir die Bilder an und beschreibe, was Anna in ihren letzten Ferien in Schottland erlebt hat.*
Verwende das simple past.

a) ....

....

b) ....

....

c) ....

....

d) ....

....

....

3. *Vervollständige den Text, indem du die Verben in die richtige Zeit setzt.*
Achte auf die Signalwörter!

My family .... (live) in London. Our house .... (be) very old. My grandmother always .... (say) that there is a ghost in the bedroom upstairs. She can often .... (hear) the ghost at night. Last year, the ghost .... (speak) to her. My grandmother .... (tell) me that story sometimes. At the moment I .... (sit) in the old bedroom and I .... (to wait) for the ghost to come and speak to me.

Verben

1

Die Zeit „dazwischen“ – present perfect

Eine Form, mit deren Hilfe Vergangenheit und Gegenwart in Verbindung gebracht werden können, ist das simple present perfect. Immer wenn du einen Bezug zur Gegenwart herstellen möchtest, verwendest du das simple present perfect. Wenn du ausdrücken möchtest, wann etwas in der Vergangenheit geschehen ist, verwendest du simple past tense. Es gibt drei Einsatzmöglichkeiten.

Erstens: Wenn du von einem Vorgang sprichst, der in der **Vergangenheit angefangen hat und bis in die Gegenwart andauert**.

Tom has lived in London since the year 2010.

Zweitens: Wenn du von einer Handlung oder einem Ereignis sprichst, welches zwar **schon beendet, aber immer noch wirksam ist**.

The streets are wet. It has rained!

Drittens: Wenn du über Handlungen oder Ereignisse sprichst, die unmittelbar vorher, also „gerade eben“, stattgefunden haben.

Ben has just come home.

Wie wird das simple present perfect gebildet?

Zeit	Verb Aussagesatz	Frage	Verneinung
simple present perfect	have + -ed (regelmäßige Verben) oder + 3. Form (unregelmäßige Verben). Bei he/she/it has + -ed/ 3. Form. **I have bought a car. She has come home.**	Subjekt zwischen have/has und der perfect form. **Has he finished his homework? Have you seen Anna?**	haven't/ hasn't + -ed oder 3. Form **He hasn't seen her. You haven't eaten yet.**

Tipp:
Signalwörter sind: **since** (Zeitpunkt), **for** (Zeitspanne), **never**, **ever** **yet** (noch nicht), **just** (gerade eben), **already** (schon).

2

1. *Bilde die simple-present-perfect-Form und die Frageform.*

a) to play I ....

.... ?

b) to go She.. .

.... ?

c) to be You.. .

.... ?

d) to become He.. .

.... ?

e) to visit We.. .

.... ?

2. *Sage auf Englisch, dass …*

a) du noch nie in Amerika warst. ....

....

b) du gerade eben deine Hände gewaschen hast. ....

....

c) sie Ben gesehen hat. ....

....

3. *Frage auf Englisch, ob…*

a) er jemals in Afrika war. ....

....

b) Tina seit fünf Jahren in Brighton lebt. ....

....

Verben

c) Jimmy seit 2013 Rugby spielt. ....

....

4. *Finde die Fehler bei den Signalwörtern und korrigiere.*

a) The cat has slept since two hours. ....

....

b) I haven't done my homework already. ....

....

c) Has she been to England never? ....

....

5. *Setze die Verben in der richtigen Form ein: simple past oder simple present perfect.*

Carla has got a friend in America. She .... (to want) to visit her for three years now.

Last week Carla .... (to arrive) in New York. On her first day Carla .... (to be) very excited about all the interesting things you can see and do in New York!

She .... (not/to be) to the Empire State Building, yet, but she .... already .... (to see) some important sights of New York.

A few days ago her host-family .... (to take) her to visit a famous museum, the Museum of Modern Art and Carla .... (to love) the paintings she saw there.

Yesterday morning her mother called her from Germany.

“Tell me about the things you .... (to do) since last week!” she said. Carla told her everything.

“We .... just .... (to book) some tickets for Disney World!” she said, “I am so excited!”

Test

3

1. *Carla ist seit einigen Tagen bei ihrer Freundin in New York zu Gast. Sie hat eine Checkliste für Sehenswürdigkeiten. Was hat sie bereits erledigt und was noch nicht? Benutze das simple present perfect und schreibe die Sätze in dein Heft.*

- ☑ visit Modern Art Museum
- ☐ take pictures of Empire State Building
- ☑ spend some time at the New York Zoo
- ☑ visit Statue of Liberty
- ☐ go to Disney World

2. *Finde die Frage zur Antwort.*

.... a cup of tea?

No, she hasn’t had a cup of tea, yet.

.... ?

Yes, I have lived in New York for five years.

.... ?

No, they haven’t bought a new car.

Verben

1

Die „Sherlock-Holmes-Zeit" – past progressive

Die Zeitform, mit deren Hilfe du über bestimmte **Momente in der Vergangenheit** sprechen kannst, ist das past progressive. Du kannst also – wie Sherlock Holmes bei seinen Ermittlungen – damit ausdrücken, dass eine Handlung in der Vergangenheit gerade im Gange war, als plötzlich etwas anderes passierte.

Im Deutschen gibt es kein past progressive. Du musst also herausfinden, ob es in der Vergangenheit um einen Zeitpunkt geht (simple past) oder einen Zeitraum (past progressive). Manchmal wird im Deutschen auch „gerade als" verwendet, um das auszudrücken, was das englische past progressive ausdrückt.

Wie wird das past progressive gebildet?

Zeit	Aussagesatz	Frage	Verneinung
past progressive	Was/were + -ing **I was watching TV when the accident happened.** **They were having dinner when the phone rang.**	Subjekt und was/were tauschen die Plätze: **Bob was sleeping** → **Was Bob sleeping?**	Was/were + not **He wasn't running.** **You weren't dreaming.**

2

1. *Gestern stahl jemand während der Sportstunde Geld aus Jojos Geldbeutel. Schreibe auf, was verschiedene Schüler gerade taten, als es geschah. Ergänze die Sätze mit den passenden Wörtern.*

to copy | to eat | to chat | to play | to look | to play

a) Benjamin .... a bar of chocolate.

b) Tina and Megan .... at a magazine.

c) Andy .... maths homework from Ben.

d) Class 6 .... basketball in the gym.

e) Anna .... with her neighbour.

Tipp:
Beachte folgende Schreibweisen.
Das stumme **-e** entfällt am Ende des Verbs.
dance – was/were dancing
Der Endkonsonant verdoppelt sich nach kurzem betonten Vokal.
stop – was/were stopping
Das **-ie** wird zu **-y(ing)**.
to lie – was/were lying

2. *Welche Sätze stehen im past progressive? Setze ein Häkchen in die entsprechenden Kästen.*

☐ The weather was changing quickly. – ☐ I stood at my window. – ☐ The storm was coming closer. – ☐ My father and my mother were searching for candles. – ☐ Jenny wasn't in her room. – ☐ Was she hiding somewhere? – ☐ Did she go outside? – ☐ When the first thunder crashed, I was calling her name. – ☐ It was getting darker and darker. – ☐ I heard footsteps behind me. – ☐ Was it Jenny? – ☐ Yes, and she was smiling at me!

3. *Sherlock Holmes befragt die Verdächtigen in einem kniffligen Fall. Vervollständige die Sätze. Beachte, dass ein Teil im past progressive stehen muss, der andere Teil aber im simple past.*

a) Mrs Nosy, ... (you/to watch) TV when you .... (to hear) the alarm?

b) Mr Roundabout, ... (your wife/to wash) her hair when you .... (to see) the young man?

c) What .... (you/to do) in the living room, Mr Careless?

Verben

d) .... (the maid/to clean) the windows when you .... (to hear) the scream, Lady Goosebumps?

e) Butler James, where .... (to be/ Mr and Mrs White) when you .... (to be) speaking to the stranger?

f) Mr and Mrs White, ... (you/to play) the piano together when Butler James .... (to come) in?

4. *Was passierte, während der Unhold sein Unwesen trieb? Bilde jeweils zwei Sätze und achte darauf, die Angaben mit einem Kreuz zu verneinen. Schreibe in dein Heft.*

a) Will	to sleep in his bed ☒	to stand at the window ☑
b) The wind	to howl ☑	to blow softly ☒
c) The dog	to hide under the bed ☑	to sleep in front of the fireplace ☒
d) The cat	to hunt mice ☒	to sit on Will's bed. ☑

5. *Was taten die anderen während dieser Zeit? Frage nach den unterstrichenen Satzteilen.*

a) Grandma and Grandpa were helping <u>their neighbour</u>.

....?

b) <u>Jessica</u> was cooking noodles.

....?

c) Anna was sleeping <u>in her bed</u>.

....?

d) The children were playing cards.

....?

6. *In der 6. Klasse wurde gestern ein Gastschüler aus Afrika begrüßt. Auf einmal ertönte der Feueralarm. Schreibe auf, was die anderen Schüler und Lehrer zu dieser Zeit gerade taten.*

a) Mr Cooper .... (talk) to some girls from class 5.

b) James, John and Jordan .... (play basketball).

c) Bridget .... (write) a math test.

d) Class 8 .... (watch) a DVD about the life of whales.

e) Mrs Nelson .... (look) for Simon.

7. *Sage auf Englisch, dass …*

a) du dein Zimmer aufgeräumt hast, während deine Mutter einkaufen war.

....

....

b) deine Eltern einen Film sahen, als du das Geräusch hörtest.

....

....

8. *Frage auf Englisch, ob …*

a) Ben im Wohnzimmer war, als das Licht ausging.

....

....

Verben

b) Sherlock Holmes eine Pfeife rauchte, als Watson ihn traf.

....

....

c) die Katze Milch trank, als der Hund ins Haus kam.

....

....

9. *Finde die Fehler und korrigiere den ganzen Satz.*

a) She played in the garden while he cooked lunch.

....

....

b) Mrs Donovan watching TV when the storm began.

....

....

c) Mr Donovan were reading a book when the storm was beginning.

....

....

10. *Richtig oder falsch? Kreuze an.*

	R	F
a) They was in the classroom, when the fire alarm went off.	☐	☐
b) She read a book, when he came home.	☐	☐

Test

1. *Der afrikanische Gastschüler Gregory verwechselt oft die Namen der neuen Mitschüler. Erkläre ihm, welcher Mitschüler was tat, als gestern der Feueralarm losging.*

a) Gregory: “Was Sandy doing her homework? “

You: “No, ... Anna

....”

b) Gregory: “Were Luka and Noel eating sandwiches? ”

You: “No, ... Hannes and Christian

....”

c) Gregory: “Was Noah talking to his friends?”

You: “No, ... Helena ....

....”

2. *Der Direktor befragt Schüler, um herauszufinden, wer den Feueralarm ausgelöst hat. Schreibe die Antworten der Schüler.*

Mr. Simons: “What were you doing when the fire alarm went off?“ Pascal: “ ....

.... ”

(daydream about favorite rock star)

Louisa: “ .... ”

(look at my fingernails)

Tom: “ .... ”

(try to solve personal problem)

Raffael: “ .... ”

(stand in front of fire alarm button)

Verben

1

Die Zeiten der Zukunft – will-future and going-to-future

Es gibt im Englischen zwei Zeitformen, mit deren Hilfe du Zukünftiges ausdrücken kannst. Das will-future verwendest du, wenn du über zukünftige Ereignisse sprechen möchtest, **die du nicht beeinflussen kannst**. Das going-to-future **drückt dagegen eine Absicht, ein Vorhaben aus**. Es kann auch ausdrücken, dass etwas demnächst oder in unmittelbarer Zukunft geschehen wird.

Wie werden will-future und going-to-future gebildet?

Zeit	Verb Aussagesatz	Frage	Verneinung
will-future	will + Grundform **It will rain today.** **They will be here by 12 o'clock.**	Subjekt und will tauschen die Plätze: **Bob will sing → Will Bob sing?**	will + not = won't **He won't go out.**
going-to-future	to be + going to + Grundform **I am going to be a star.** **She is going to laugh.**	Subjekt und am/is/are tauschen die Plätze: **I am going to be a star.** **Am I going to be a star?**	am/is/are + not **She isn't going to laugh.**

2

1. *Auf dem Jahrmarkt trifft Anna eine Wahrsagerin, die ihr aus der Hand liest. Hier sind deren Voraussagen. Verwende das will-future und die Verben aus den Kästchen.*

find | fall in love | not have | meet | travel | change

a) Ah, Anna, you .... around the world.

b) At first, you .... a lot of money, but then things .... for the better.

c) You .... the perfect job.

d) In Paris you .... a handsome, young man.

e) He .... with you.

Tipp:
Ein typischer Fehler ist das Verwechseln von **will** und **want to**
Beachte:

Ich will = I want (to) **Ich will nicht = I don't want (to)**
Ich werde = I will/I am going to
Ich werde nicht = I won't/I am not going to

2. *Anna schlendert über den Jahrmarkt. Setze will-future oder going-to-future ein.*

a) I think I .... (buy) more chocolate ice-cream.

b) Oh, I have eaten too much. I am afraid I ....
(be sick)!

c) I .... (not go) on the roller coaster
(Achterbahn).

d) Tonight I .... (drink) chamomile tea.

e) Oh, look at that man spitting fire! He ....
(burn) himself!

f) Oh, they also sell candy floss (Zuckerwatte). I am feeling better
already, so I .... (have) some.

3. *Sage auf Englisch, dass …*

a) du glaubst, dass es regnen wird.

....

b) du vorhast, auf ein Geburtstagsfest zu gehen.

....

Verben

4. *Frage auf Englisch, ob …*

a) Anna vorhat, in die Geisterbahn (ghost train) zu gehen.

....

b) Pascal keine Angst haben wird.

....

c) Anna noch einen Hamburger essen wird.

....

d) deine Eltern dich abholen werden.

....

5. *Vervollständige die Sätze mithilfe der richtigen Verneinung.*

a) The roller coaster looks scary so I .... (not go) up.

b) The cotton floss (Zuckerwatte) is delicious but Anna .... (not have more).

6. *Lies die Sätze und streiche die falsche Form durch.*

a) I feel terrible. I think I **am going to/will** be sick.
b) Look at those clouds! It **is going to/will** rain any minute.
c) We have a free evening so we **are going to/will** see Shrek.
d) Do you think Luka **is going to/will** visit us today?
e) I am easily scared, so I **am not going to/won't** go on the ghost train.

7. *Verneine die Sätze und schreibe sie in dein Heft.*

a) John will hurt himself.
b) Eliza is going to meet her friend tomorrow.

Test

1. *Markiere die Fehler.*

a) The ghost train is going to be scary.

b) She want go on the roller coaster.

c) We is going to see the new movie.

d) It is going to rain.

2. *Sieh Dir die Bilder an und schreibe auf, was Anna sich für ihre Zukunft vorstelllt.*

a) ....

....

b) ....

....

c) ....

....

d) ....

....

....

3. *Verneine die Sätze in deinem Heft.*

a) He will find the keys.

b) It will snow soon.

c) They are going to buy me a present.

Verben

1

Die Vorvergangenheit – past perfect

Das past perfect ist eine Zeitform, mit deren Hilfe du einen **Zeitpunkt in der Vergangenheit beschreiben kannst, der noch vor einem anderen lag**, das „Vorgestern" sozusagen. Dabei betonst du nicht die Handlung, sondern die Tatsache, dass es eben vor einem anderen bereits vergangenen Zeitpunkt geschehen ist.
Du musst immer gut überlegen, was zuerst passierte. Das erste Ereignis steht im past perfect („vorgestern"), das zweite Ereignis („gestern") steht im simple past.

Before I came here I had spoken to Jillian.
After I had spoken to Jillian, I came here.

Wie wird das simple past perfect gebildet?

Zeit	Aussagesatz	Frage	Verneinung
past perfect	had + -ed (bei regelmäßigen Verben) oder + 3. Verform/past participle (bei unregelmäßige Verben). **I had bought a car before the accident happened.**	Subjekt zwischen have/has und der perfect form. **Had he finished his homework before he left?**	had + not + -ed oder 3. Verbform **He hadn't seen her. You hadn't eaten.**

Tipp:
Signalwörter können **before** (vorher) und **after** (danach) und **when** (als) sein.

2

1. *Setze das Verb im past perfect ein.*

a) My bike .... (disappear).

b) Our coach .... (help) us.

c) The championship .... (be) lost.

d) Her tennis racket .... (broken).

e) The horse .... (won) the race.

f) The Stuntman .... (lost) his nerve.

2. *Löse das Kreuzworträtsel, indem du die past-participle-Form (3. Verbform) des Verbs einträgst.*

senkrecht
1 come
2 find
3 catch
4 draw

waagrecht
1 be
2 dig
3 cut
4 forget

	1		2					
					3			
								4
1								
			2					
4								

3. *Verwende die Sätze aus Aufgabe 1 jeweils in verneinendem Sinn.*

a) My bike had not disappeared when I came out of the shop.

b) ....

before we went into camp.

c) ....

when they scored the first goal.

d) ....

before she finished the match.

Verben

4. *Sage auf Englisch, dass …*

a) dein Training noch nicht beendet war, als du nach Hause gingst.

....

b) das Team verloren hatte, bevor das Foul passierte.

....

c) du den Ball zu Ben geworfen hast, nachdem du ihn gefangen hattest.

....

d) du die neuen Regeln gekannt hattest, bevor du ins Spiel kamst (to enter the game).

....

e) es zu regnen anfing, nachdem du das Schwimmbad verlassen hattest.

....

f) Sam dich gewarnt hatte, bevor du dich verletzt hast (to hurt yourself).

....

3 Test

1. *Bilde die past-participle-Formen.*

a) to eat ....
b) to bite ....
c) to draw ....
d) to think ....
e) to catch ....
f) to forget ....
g) to chose ....
h) to become ....

2. *Vervollständige die Sätze im past perfect.*

a) Tom .... (go out) when his girlfriend called.

b) .... he .... (leave) a message for her?

c) No, he .... (write) a note, before he left.

d) .... she .... (be) angry about that?

e) Yes, she .... (be) angry at first.

f) But when she saw, what he .... (buy) her, she smiled.

3. *Simple past oder past perfect?*

a) After we .... (see) the finals of the football championship in Brazil, we .... (to fly) back home.

b) My mother .... (book) our flights before we .... (leave) for the finals.

c) We .... (arrive) at the airport, when Mum .... (start) looking for the tickets.

d) She .... (put) everything in her handbag, but now she .... (can) not find them.

d) My father .... (watch) her for a while, before he.................................... (say): "I have the tickets in my jacket, because I did not want you to lose them."

1.4 Modalverben

1

can, can't, must, mustn't, need, needn't

Um auszudrücken, dass jemand etwas **kann** oder zu etwas in der Lage ist, verwendest du im Englischen can.
Um auszudrücken, dass jemand etwas **tun muss**, verwendest du must. Aber aufgepasst: **must not (mustn't)** bedeutet etwas **nicht dürfen** (Verbot). Mit **need not (needn't)** drückst du aus, dass jemand etwas **nicht tun muss**.
Nach **can, must, needn't** steht das Verb in der Grundform.

I can swim.	Ich kann schwimmen. Ich bin in der Lage zu schwimmen.
I can't swim.	Ich kann nicht schwimmen. Ich bin nicht in der Lage zu schwimmen.
I must go.	Ich muss gehen.
I needn't go.	Ich muss nicht gehen.
I mustn't go.	Ich darf nicht gehen.

2

1. *Wähle das richtige Modalverb aus und vervollständige den Text.*

I .... stay at home today because I am sick. The doctor said I .... go to school. He said that I .... stay in bed the whole time. But I .... do too much, because my head hurts. So I .... to wait until I feel better before I can go out to meet my friends.

2. *Sage auf Englisch, dass …*

a) du heute keine Hausaufgaben machen brauchst.

....

b) wir Fußball spielen können.

....

c) er dieses Match gewinnen muss.

....

d) Tim nicht nach draussen darf.

....

e) ich das nicht tun kann.

....

3. *Wähle das richtige Modalverb aus und vervollständige die Sätze.*

a) You .... stay in bed, because you are very sick!

b) She .... stay in bed, because she has to go to school.

c) I .... stay in bed, because the doctor said I should go for walks.

d) We .... stay in bed, because it's Sunday.

e) They .... stay in bed, because it's Monday morning!

4. *Finde die Fehler und korrigiere den ganzen Satz.*

a) I can playing the piano.

....

b) We mustn't do any homework today.

....

c) I cann't sing well.

....

Verben

5. *Christians Eltern sind übers Wochenende weggefahren. Er und sein Bruder Joe sind allein zu Hause. Schau dir Übersicht mit den Verboten und dem Erlaubten an und bilde Sätze.*

Yes!	**No!**
watch TV in the afternoon	watch TV at night
eat food from the fridge	buy sweets
go to Ben's birthday party	come home after 7 o'clock
ride your bikes	go into town

a) Christian and Joe ....

but ....

b) They ....

but ....

c) They ....

but ....

d) They ....

but ....

6. *Setze das richtige Modalverb in die Lücke.*

a) Children in Great Britain .... wear school uniforms.

b) Most children in Germany .... wear school uniforms.

c) Many children in Africa .... go to school, because they are poor.

d) In some countries girls .... go to school.

Test

1. *Übersetze ins Englische.*

a) Tony kann den Test nicht schreiben, weil er Kopfschmerzen hat. ....

....

b) Ich muss 30 Minuten warten.

....

c) Sie darf den neuen Film nicht sehen.

....

2. *Wähle das richtige Modalverb aus und vervollständige den Text.*

Mum: "You .... help me with the dishes, we have a dishwasher! But go and do your homework!"

Andy: " .... I do my homework now? I want to meet Jill in five minutes!"

Mum: "No, please finish them first. Oh dear! The children .... play football on the lawn over there! Mr. Grumble will shout at them."

Andy: "I .... go and tell them and save them!"

Mum: "No, you .... You .... do your homework now. I will tell them myself."

Verben

1

have to, be allowed to, be able to

Du kannst die Modalverben can, must und needn't nur im **simple present** verwenden. Um diese Modalverben in der Vergangenheit zu verwenden, musst du sie mit **have to (müssen), be allowed to (dürfen)** oder **be able to (können, in der Lage sein)** ersetzen.
Can kann zu **could** werden.

I could hear my sister begging.

Da could aber auch verwendet wird, wenn man über eine Möglichkeit spricht, ist es oft besser, wenn du es mit **able to** oder **allowed to** ersetzt.

There could be a thunderstrom later. Es könnte später ein Gewitter geben. Vielleicht gibt es später ein Gewitter.

simple present	Verwendung	simple past Ersatzform
I can swim.	Fähigkeit	I was able to swim. I wasn't able so swim.
I must go.	Verpflichtung	I had to go.
I needn't go.	nicht müssen	I didn't have to go
I mustn't go.	Verbot	I wasn't allowed to go.

2

1. *Verbinde die deutschen Sätze mit den passenden englischen Sätzen.*

Sie darf nicht rennen.
Er kann Fahrrad fahren.
Ich muss kein Brot kaufen.
Wir müssen das sehen!
Ich kann nicht nachdenken.

I needn't buy bread.
We have to see this!
She is not allowed to run.
I can't think.
He is able to ride a bike.

2. *Ergänze die jeweils fehlende Form.*

a) Present: You needn't help me.

Past: ....

b) Present: Can the children watch a DVD?

Past: ....

c) Present: ....

Past: You weren't allowed to shout.

3. *Setze **can/can't/to be able to/must/mustn't/needn't/ to have to** sinnvoll ein. Auch Verneinungen sind möglich. Achte auf die Zeitform des Satzes!*

a) .... we have a coke? Yes, but

you ....drink it before we get on the bus.

People .... drink anything in the bus.

b) Yesterday my little sister .... pay the full prize.

Only children which are ten years and above

.... pay the full prize.

4. *Sage auf Englisch, dass …*

a) Benjamin keine Schokolade kaufen durfte.

....

b) wir einen Ausweg finden mussten.

....

c) sie nichts sagen musste.

....

5. *Finde die Fehler und korrigiere den ganzen Satz.*

a) Yesterday I must tell my parents the truth.

....

Verben

b) They are can allowed to go to the party.

....

c) She didn't have to need to run away.

....

6. *Setze die passenden Modalverben in die Lücken ein.*

Many years ago, a young man took his boat out on a lake. He .... (not swim), but he was brave (mutig). The people in his village said: "You .... take your boat on that lake! The lake monster is going to come and get you!" He knew that he .... go, but he wanted to find a treasure. He couldn't swim, but he .... to hold his breath for a very long time. "I .... find the treasure. Only then Lady Gwen will marry me!" he said to his dog. He put a rope around his dog and himself and told his dog, that he .... to run and pull when the signal came. So the young man jumped into the lake and his dog .... pull him out.

Test

1. *Übersetze die Frage und bilde die richtige Verneinung.*

a) Oh nein! Musste ich Milch kaufen? ....

....

....

b) Konntest du mit Kopfschmerzen Hausaufgaben machen?

....

....

c) Durfte Anna schwimmen gehen? ....

....

....

2. *Verbinde die Sätze mit der jeweils passenden Bedeutung.*

Are we allowed to sit here?
Visitors mustn't feed the animals.
Ben was able to run faster than Tom.

Verbot
Erlaubnis
Fähigkeit

3. *Schreibe die Sätze im simple past.*

a) I am allowed to talk to her when she comes home.

....

b) Must they brush their teeth before dinner?

....

c) I must buy bread!

....

Verben

1

may/might/should/ought to

Nun kommen zu den dir bereits bekannten Modalverben noch weitere hinzu.

simple present	Verwendung	simple past – Ersatzform
may	höfliche/formale Erlaubnis	to be allowed to
might	Möglichkeit/Vermutung	Keine Ersatzform
shall/should	Verpflichtung/Vermutung/Ratschlag	to be supposed to
ought to	wie shall/should, aber eine Verstärkung/Betonung der Aussage.	to be supposed to

2

1. *Setze die Sätze ins simple past und verwende die korrekte Ersatzform.*

a) You should do your homework now.

....

b) May she go outside with the children?

....

c) You ought to read this book for your project.

....

2. *Sage auf Englisch, dass …*

a) wir Wasser sparen sollten. (Betont!)

....

b) Alice die Königin sehen darf. (formale Erlaubnis)

....

c) Anna das Fenster öffnen sollte, um frische Luft hereinzulassen.

....

Test

1. *Welcher der beiden Sätze ist korrekt? Mache ein Häkchen.*

a) We should to leave soon. ☐
We should leave soon. ☐

b) You were supposed to go. ☐
You supposed to go. ☐

c) Liz ought call her mother. ☐
Liz ought to call her mother. ☐

2. *Schreibe im simple past.*

a) We ought to take off our shoes in here.

....

b) Should we tell father about the test?

....

c) You ought to apologize!

....

3. *Sage auf Englisch, dass …*

a) Emma sich hinsetzen darf. (Formale Erlaubnis)

....

b) Jessica zuhören sollte. (Betont!)

....

c) wir das nicht tun sollten. (Ratschlag)

....

1.5 Gerund

1

Gerund als Subjekt oder Objekt

Du findest im Englischen Verben, die sich wie Nomen „benehmen“ können. Sie sind von der Grundform des Verbs abgeleitet und mit einer -ing-Endung versehen. Diese „substantivierten“ Verben heißen Gerund. Das Gerund kann Subjekt oder Objekt im Satz sein.

Smoking is not allowed.	Jane loves reading.
Gerund als Subjekt	Gerund als Objekt

Tipp:
Nach Verben, die Gefühle ausdrücken, musst du oft ein Gerund verwenden. **like, love, enjoy, hate, can't stand** …
In diesen Fällen ist das Gerund Objekt des Satzes.

2

1. *Schreibe die Bedeutung der Schilder auf. Verwende das Gerund.*

a)  ....

b)  ....

c)  ....

2. *Übertrage ins Englische.*

a) Anna liebt Tanzen.

....

b) Ich mag Wandern (wandern = to hike) nicht.

....

3. *Vervollständige die Sätze mithilfe des Gerund.*

a) .... in bed on a Sunday morning is wonderful. (to stay)

b) Anna loves .... Her cakes are very good. (to bake)

c) I like .... sports but I think .... is horrible. (to do / to cycle)

4. *Sage auf Englisch, dass … Schreibe in dein Heft.*

a) Basketball spielen dein Hobby ist.
b) du gerne liest.
c) du Angeln langweilig findest.

Test

3

1. *Unterstreiche das Gerund.*

a) Swimming is fun.
b) Benjamin and Finn like playing computer games.

2. *Finde den Fehler und korrigiere den ganzen Satz! Schreibe in dein Heft.*

a) Peter and Tom can't stand dance.
b) They think to dancing is stupid.
c) But Sophie loves dance.
d) Played football is her other hobby.

Verben

1

Gerund nach Präpositionen

Im Englischen gibt es Adjektive, die mit **to be** und **einer Präposition** verbunden sind.

to be interested in reading ...

Nach solchen Verbindungen verwendest du das Gerund. Hier findest du einige dieser Adjektive.

to be afraid of (Angst haben vor etwas)	to be sorry about/for (Mitleid/Leid empfinden wegen etwas)
to be bad at/to be good at (gut/schlecht sein in etwas)	to be tired of (leid sein, etwas zu tun)
to be excited about (wegen etwas aufgeregt sein)	to be used to (gewohnt sein, etwas zu tun)
to be happy about (glücklich sein über etwas)	to be interested in (an etwas interessiert sein)

2

1. *Was können diese Jugendlichen gut? Verwende das Gerund.*

a)

....

b)

....

c)

....

2. *Unterstreiche das Adjektiv mit Präposition und das Gerund.*

a) I was afraid of losing my way.
b) She was sorry about breaking that window.
c) We were tired of talking about the problem.
d) Are you interested in buying this smartphone?

3. *Tim hat viele Interessen und Hobbies und mag anderes gar nicht.*
Bilde Sätze und verwende die entsprechenden Adjektive mit Präposition sowie Gerund. Schreibe in dein Heft.

Tim → climb, snakes and other reptiles ☺
→ horse riding, mice ☹

Test

3

1. *Verwende das Gerund. Sage auf Englisch, dass …*
Schreibe in dein Heft.

a) du aufgeregt bist, weil du nach Paris gehst.
b) du Angst hast, Schlangen zu sehen.
c) sie es leid ist, dir zuzuhören.
d) Ben sich freut, Anna zu treffen.

2. *Finde den Fehler und korrigiere den ganzen Satz.*
Achte auf die Präpositionen.

a) My father is used working in the garden.
b) Luka is good at make people smile.
c) We are interested in to sail.

2. Präpositionen

1

Zeitangaben: Tagesdatum, Monate und Jahre

Monate und Wochentage werden im Englischen immer groß-geschrieben.

Die Wochentage:
Monday, Tuesday, Wednesday, Thursday, Friday, Saturday, Sunday.

Die Monate:
January, February, March, April, May, June, July, August, September, October, November, December

Welche Präposition gehört zu welcher Zeitangabe?
Schau Dir die Tabelle an:

Tagesangaben und genaue Datumsangaben, Tageszeiten **My birthday is on February, 28th.**	on
bei Monats- und Jahresangaben **I will fly to London in September. I was born in 2005.** bei Tageszeiten (morgens, nachmittags) **in the morning, in the afternoon**	in
bestimmte Zeitpunkte (z. B. Uhrzeiten, Feiertage, nachts) **at breakfast, at 12 o'clock, at Christmast, at night**	at

Tipp:
Amerikanisches Englisch: **on** the weekend
Britisches Englisch: **at** the weekend

2

1. *Füge die korrekte Präposition ein.*

a) I was born .... 2003.

b) Can we meet .... Monday?

Tipp:
Bei genauen Tages- und Datumsangaben brauchst du keinen Artikel. Das ist im Deutschen anders!
Heute ist der 4. September → Today it is September, 4th.

2. *Sage auf Englisch, dass … Schreibe in dein Heft.*

a) Sabrina am 24. März Geburtstag hat.

b) dein Vater 1975 geboren wurde.

3. *Ergänze den Kalender.*

Monday		Wednesday		Friday	Saturday	Sunday

January	February		
May		July	August
September		November	December

Test

3

1. *Sage auf Englisch, dass … Schreibe in dein Heft.*

a) du am Wochenende deine Tante besuchst.

b) Ben im Moment keine Zeit hat.

c) du morgens Tee trinkst.

2. *Finde den Fehler und korrigiere den ganzen Satz. Schreibe in dein Heft.*

a) I can't sleep in the night.

b) Today is the September, 5th.

c) We are in France on August.

Präpositionen

1

Zeitangaben und Ortsangaben

Manche Zeitangaben zeigen einen Zeitraum oder Zeitpunkt an, der in der Vergangenheit liegt.

during During the storm it was dark.	während
ago Ceasar lived more than 2000 years ago.	vor … Jahren etc.
before Wash your hands before you eat.	zuvor, davor
since (Zeitpunkt)/for (Zeitspanne) I have lived here since 2005. I have lived here for 9 years.	seit

Tipp:
Since oder **for**?
Mach den „lang Test“: 4 Tage lang, 3 Stunden lang, …
Wenn das geht, handelt es sich um eine Zeitspanne, das heißt du musst **for** einsetzen.

Um auszudrücken, wo sich jemand oder etwas befindet, benötigst du Präpositionen des Orts.

Präposition	**im Sinne von**
at Luisa is at a concert. She is at the door. We are at the station.	**auf/bei** (bei einem Ereignis: auf einem Konzert); **an/bei** (Sie ist an der Tür. Auch im Sinne von daneben, dabei, davor); **in** (an einem Ort, der sich dadurch auszeichnet, dass man sich dort befindet, um eine konkrete Sache zu tun: Büro, Bahnhof, Kino)
in in the kitchen, in Germany, in the picture	**in** (einem Auto, Taxi; einem Raum, Gebäude, Land; einer Straße, Stadt; einem Film, Buch, einer Fernsehsendung; einer Zeitung), **auf** (einem Bild)
into (hinein)	**in** ein Gebäude oder Zimmer **hinein**
on London lies on the Thames, on the chair, on a bus, on TV	**an** (an einem Fluss), **befestigt an** (an der Mauer), **auf** (einer Seite: links, rechts; einem Stockwerk; einem Gegenstand), **in/auf** (einem öffentlichen Verkehrsmittel: Bus, Zug, Flugzeug, Fähre, **in** (Fernsehen oder Radio)

1. *Finde den Fehler und korrigiere den ganzen Satz.*

2

a) For 500 years people did not have cars.

....

b) She has played the cello since 5 years.

....

2. *Fülle die Lücken.*

a) Can you put that picture .... the wall?

b) My uncle from Australia is coming.

We are waiting .... the airport.

c) I found this picture .... a magazine.

Test

3

Fülle die Lücken.

Dear Grandma, we have been in London .... last Monday and I have seen a lot! Did you know that Richard Lionheart lived almost a 1000 years ....? We were .... a theater to see a special show about him and the people of his time. Posters about this show were .... every bus and train. .... the show Dad had to go to the restrooms, because he forgot to go .... the show. Mum was angry with him! And did you know that London is .... the Thames? That river is quite smelly!

Yours Anna

Präpositionen

1

Ortsangaben und Richtungsangaben

Um Orte, Positionen und Richtung anzugeben, benötigst du Präpositionen.

Präposition	im Sinne von
by/next to/beside The king stands beside his queen.	**daneben**
over fly over the ocean, jump over the fence, put your hand over your mouth	**über** (wenn etwas anderes bedeckt wird, auf die andere Seite gelangen (auch *across*), über ein höheres Hindernis)
across She travelled across America.	**über, durch** (auf die andere Seite gelangen)
through Don't dive through the tunnel!	**hindurch** (Begrenzung nötig, etwa oben und an den Seiten bei einem Tunnel oder klar umrissende Region/ Gegend: durch die Wüste hindurch)
from I am from Germany.	**von/aus** (von einem Ort, von einer Person)
onto She climbed onto the roof.	**auf** (etwas hinauf)
to Give it to Tom. Let's go to Paris! Go to bed!	**zu** (einem Gebäude, einer Person), **in** (einen Ort, in ein Land, ins Bett gehen)

2

1. *Finde den Fehler und korrigiere den ganzen Satz.*

a) My father walked over the desert.

....

b) Lucy is of England.

....

2. *Fülle die Lücken mit der entsprechenden Präposition.*

a) If you want to get there, you must climb .... the wall.

b) The hospital is .... the parking lot.

c) I said .... him: "Be quiet!"

3. *Vervollständige diese Ausdrücke mithilfe der entsprechenden Präpositionen.*

a) to travel .... the world

b) pick up fast food at a drive-..........

c) letters .... Julia.

Test

3

1. *Fülle die Lücken im Text, indem du die richtigen Präpositionen einsetzt.*

Dear diary, yesterday I got a funny, old box .... my mum. She told me that it was very, very old. Kings and queens had carried it .... the country. There was a strange stone inside and .... the stone lay a blue cloth. I took out the cloth and the stone and put the stone .... the cloth – but it didn't stay there. It always flew off the cloth and finally landed .... my foot. When I went .... bed, I took the stone with me. But this morning the stone cracked open and suddenly there was a funny little animal .... me. I named it Arthur and he is my secret. I won't give him .... anyone else!

2. *Finde den Fehler und korrigiere den ganzen Satz. Achte auf die Präpositionen. Schreibe in dein Heft.*

a) The little animal was besides me.

b) Somebody put a cloth to the stone.

c) I went in bed and the stone cracked.

3. Nomen

1

Groß- und Kleinschreibung

Im Englischen werden fast alle Wörter kleingeschrieben.
Ausnahmen sind:
Ich: **I** (wird immer großgeschrieben, auch wenn es mitten im Satz steht!)
Satzanfang: **She loves horses.**
Gruß und Schlußformel im Brief: **Dear … Yours …**
Eigennamen und Titel: **Ben, Anna, Robin Hood, Mr, Mrs …**
Länder und Sprachen: **England, English, France, French**
Himmelsrichtungen: **East, West, South, North**
Wochentage und Monate: **Monday, August**

2

1. *Finde die Fehler und korrigiere den ganzen Satz.*

a) What do i want?

……………………………………………………………………………………

b) Do you speak german?

……………………………………………………………………………………

c) Jo loves cats. but she hates spiders.

……………………………………………………………………………………

2. *Sage auf Englisch, dass …*

a) du in England wohnst.

……………………………………………

……………………………………………

b) Tom und Susie deine Freunde sind.

……………………………………………………………………………………

3. *Welche dieser Wörter schreibt man im Englischen groß? Markiere sie*

horse book i queen tarzan
you england german boy

4. *Nun bilde vier Sätze, in denen jeweils eines dieser markierten Wörter vorkommt.*

....

....

....

....

....

....

Test

3

Korrigiere diesen Text.

this is mr jones. He lives in london. He has a daughter, emma, and a son, tom. They all like to go to the north of Scotland because they have a castle there.

....

....

....

....

....

....

Nomen

1

Pluralformen

Die Mehrzahl (Plural) bildest du, indem du ein s an die Einzahlform (Singularform) hängst. Dabei gelten folgende Regeln:

regelmäßige Bildung: -s	one cat – two cats, one house – two houses, a car – five cars
Nomen, die auf **Konsonant + y** enden: -ies	one baby – two babies, one family – three families
Nomen, die auf **-f** oder **-fe** enden: -ves	one wife – six wives, a knife – two knives
Nomen, die auf einen **Zischlaut** enden: -es	one box – two boxes

Es gibt allerdings einige wenige Substantive mit unregelmäßigen Pluralformen. Hier eine Auswahl häufiger Wörter:

one man	**two men**	**one woman**	**two women**
one child	**two children**	**one foot**	**two feet**
one tooth	**two teeth**	**one mouse**	**two mice**
one sheep	**two sheep**	**one fish**	**two fish**

Diese unregelmäßigen Formen musst du auswendig lernen.

2

1. *Finde die Pluralformen, markiere sie und schreibe sie auf.*

S	P	A	R	T	S	F
T	E	E	T	H	K	D
D	O	N	U	I	L	F
H	P	Q	T	M	M	I
J	L	A	D	I	E	S
L	E	W	R	C	N	H
O	M	Y	F	E	V	E

a) part ....

b) people ....

c) tooth ....

d) lady ....

e) fish ....

f) mouse ....

g) man ....

Tipp:
Es gibt auch Nomen, die nur in der Mehrzahl verwendet werden.
clothes, glasses, jeans, pyjamas, people, police, scissors, shorts, trousers

2. *Sieh dir die Bilder an und schreibe auf, was du siehst.*

a) 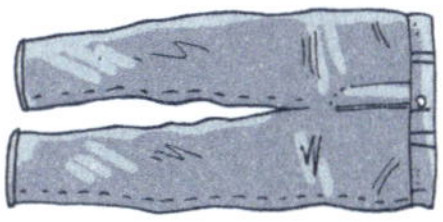
....

b) 
....

c) 
....

d) 
....

e) 
....

Tipp:
This wird zu **these** (Dinge/Personen, die sich nah befinden)
That wird zu **those** (Dinge/Personen, die weiter entfernt sind)

3. *Setze this/ these richtig ein.*

a) .... is my new friend Rajan.

b) .... are my new shoes.

c) .... exercises are not easy!

d) .... boy is friendly.

Nomen

4. *Sieh dir Kathys neue Dinge an und die alten.*

a) .... is Kathy's new dress and .... are Kathy's old jeans.

b) .... is Kathy's new bag and .... are her old backpacks.

c) ....

d) ....

5. *Richtig oder Falsch? Kreuze an.*

	R	F
a) These man is a thief!	☐	☐
b) This are not my books!	☐	☐
c) These are my new jeans.	☐	☐

Test

1. *Wie lautet die Einzahl?*

a) men ....

b) police ....

c) families ....

2. *Bilde die Pluralformen.*

a) woman ....

b) window ....

c) hobby ....

d) shoe ....

e) hour ....

3. *Sage auf Englisch, dass ...*

a) zwei Kinder im Garten spielen.

....

b) dein Freund viele Fische hat.

....

c) weiße Mäuse hübscher sind als graue Mäuse.

....

Nomen

1

Pluralformen: one, ones

Um ein zählbares Nomen nicht wiederholen zu müssen, kannst du **one** oder **ones** verwenden.

Sieh dir die Beispiele in der Tabelle an:

one	Which **DVD** would you like to watch? The new **one**, please!
ones	I like your new **jeans**. I liked the old **ones** better.

2

1. *Ersetze die unterstrichenen Satzteile mit **one** oder **ones**.*

a) I would like to buy those shoes. – The red <u>shoes</u>?

b) Where is my bag? – The new <u>bag</u> or the old <u>bag</u>?

2. *Fülle die Lücken mit **one** oder **ones**.*

a) If you want comfortable shoes, take those ....

b) Look at that old car! – Which ....? – That ....!

c) Ben loves marshmellows. He likes the white .... best.

3. ***one** oder **ones**? Kreuze an.*

a) the red apples	one ☐	ones ☐
b) the green bird	one ☐	ones ☐
c) the round glasses	one ☐	ones ☐

4. *Finde die Fehler und korrigiere den ganzen Satz.*

a) I like my new hairstyle! I liked the old ones better.

....

....

b) She bought the wrong apples because I can't eat

the green one. ....

....

Test

3

1. *Fülle die Lücken im Text, indem du **one** oder **ones** einsetzt.*

Linda: "Mum, I saw really great shoes yesterday!"

Ben: "Oh no, mum! She is talking about the ugly ...."

Linda: "They were great! That T-shirt you bought was ugly."

Ben: "Are you talking about the black ....?"

Linda: "Yes, that .... The .... we saw at the other shop were much nicer."

2. *Ersetze die unterstrichenen Satzteile mit **one** oder **ones**.*

a) The apples over there look really good. – The green apples?

....

b) I like my new teachers, but Mrs Jones is the best. – Is she the good-looking teacher?

....

c) Please give me that photo. – The black and white photo?

....

3. *one oder ones? Kreuze an.*

a) the two blue fish — one ☐ ones ☐
b) one black sheep — one ☐ ones ☐
c) the red shoes — one ☐ ones ☐

Nomen

1

Genitiv: Possessive 's

Wenn du ausdrücken möchtest, dass etwas einer Person oder einem Tier mit Namen gehört, verwendest du im Englischen den 's-Genitiv. Dazu schreibst du den Namen oder die Bezeichnung in der Einzahl und hängst ein 's an.

Das Auto von Luka/Lukas Auto – Luka's car.
Das Futter von (Kater) Garfield/Garfields Futter – Garfield's food

Tipp:
Im Deutschen wird der Genitiv auch mit s gebildet. Im Normalfall allerdings ohne Apostroph. **Peter's Auto** ist im Deutschen falsch. Es muss heißen **Peters Auto**.

Bei Substantiven (nouns), die den **Plural nicht mit -s bilden**, hängst du zur Genitivbildung auch ein 's an.

two children – children's

2

1. *Sieh dir die Bilder an und schreibe auf, wem was gehört. Verwende den 's-Genitiv.*

a)

....

b)

....

c)

....

2. *Beantworte die Fragen mithilfe der Bilder aus Aufgabe 1.*

a) Is this Rahel's smartphone? No, ...

b) Are those Joshua's comics? No, ...

c) Is this Tom's pony? No, ...

3. *Richtig oder Falsch? Kreuze an.*

	R	F
a) These are Linda's rabbits.	☐	☐
b) I love those shoe's.	☐	☐
c) Look at this test! Is it Ben's?	☐	☐

Test

3

1. *Ergänze die Lücken mit Plural-s oder 's-Genitiv.*

Nelly and Louisa are shopping. They are looking at the shop window........

Nelly........ mobile phone rings. Her mother wants to know where she is. Louisa........ mother knows that the girl........ are in town.

Nelly........ sister forgot to tell their mother.

2. *Sage auf Englisch, dass …*

a) das Toms Jacke ist.

....

b) es in deiner Straße viele Autos gibt.

....

c) Sams Mutter nett ist.

....

Nomen

1

Possessive Plural, 's-Genitiv oder of-Genitiv

Wenn du ein Genitiv-s an ein Wort anhängen möchtest, das im **Plural** steht, dann bleibt das Plural -s am Wort stehen und du hängst nur das ' (Apostroph) an.

Der Lehrer der Schüler → the pupils' teacher
Die Bücher meiner Schwestern → my sisters' books.

Tipp:
Bei unregelmäßigen Pluralformen (siehe Seite 72) hängst du ein ganz normales **'s** an.

the men's clothes
the children's toys

Nun kann es sein, dass es sich nicht um eine Person handelt, der etwas gehört, sondern um eine Sache, ein Ding oder einen Begriff. In diesem Fall verwendest du den **of-Genitiv**. **Du hängst kein -'s** an, du nutzt vielmehr eine Konstruktion mit of.

the window of the house
the back of the car
the top of my head

2

1. *Bilde erst den Singular und dann den Plural im 's-Genitiv.*

a) one brother – books ....

two brothers – books ....

b) one child – tent ....

four children – tents ....

c) one pupil – pen ....

ten pupils – pens ....

2. *Richtig oder falsch? Kreuze an.*

	R	F
a) The front of the house.	☐	☐
b) The shoe's colour.	☐	☐
c) The girl's smile.	☐	☐

3. *Finde die passenden Paare und bilde den of-Genitiv*

cake	surprise	....
tree	candles	the leaves of the tree
day	size	....
present	leaves	....

4. *Fülle die Lücke und entscheide ob 's-Genitiv oder of-Genitiv.*

a) .... sat around a round table.

(King Arthur/knights)

b) The .... (table/colour) was gold.

c) The .... (queen/dress) was silver.

d) .... (castle/size) was huge.

e) The black prince was the ....

(people/fear)

5. *Sage auf Englisch, dass...*

a) die Ferien der Familie Jones furchtbar waren.

....

b) die Farbe des neuen Autos furchtbar ist.

....

Nomen

c) die Geschenke der Kinder teuer waren.

....

d) die Augen der Katzen grün waren.

....

6. *Benutze jeweils ein Wort aus der rechten und linken Spalte, um auszudrücken, was zusammengehört. Entscheide, ob **'s-** oder **of-Genitiv** verwendet werden muss.*

boy	bag	....
pupils	lesson	....
children	holidays	....
map	Germany	....
girls	textbooks	....

7. *Finde die Fehler und korrigiere den ganzen Satz.*

a) The dress of the queen was beautiful.

....

b) The kings eyes were closed.

....

c) The mens's laughter was loud.

....

Test

1. *Finde die Fehler und korrigiere den ganzen Satz.*

a) The ladies’s dresses looked lovely.

....

b) The castle’s gardens were beautiful.

....

c) The prince’s eyes’ were shining, when he saw the lady.

....

....

2. *Sage auf Englisch, dass …*

a) das Auto deiner Eltern neu ist.

....

b) die neue Uniform der Schüler gut aussieht.

....

c) die Fenster des alten Hauses kaputt sind.

....

3. *’s-Genitiv oder of-Genitiv?*

a) book/page ....

b) Linda/dog ....

c) teacher/bag ....

d) shoes/sole ....

Nomen

1

Besonderheiten des 's-Genitiv und Ortsangaben mit 's-Genitiv

Den 's-Genitiv verwendest du auch bei Ortsangaben, wenn dein Zielort durch eine Berufsgruppe (z. B. Ärzte) oder eine Person (z. B. deine Tante) definiert wird.

I went to the doctor's (office). Let's go to Sarah's (house).

Bei diesen Sätzen werden die in Klammer gesetzen Worte „mitgedacht".

Bei mehreren „Besitzern", die hintereinander genannt werden, wird nur der zweite apostrophiert.

Tom and Brenda's dog is very old.

Bei **Eigennamen**, die auf ein -s enden, hat man zwei Möglichkeiten: Entweder kennzeichnet man den Genitiv lediglich durch den Apostroph oder man hängt auch hier **'s** an.

James' car is brand new. – James's car is brand new.

2

1. *Entscheide welcher 's-Genitiv eingesetzt werden muss.*

a) Becky .... two dogs are crazy.

b) The Burtons .... children are nice.

c) Are the children .... bags in the classroom?

d) Lars .... teacher is very nice.

2. *Setze den 's-Genitiv oder das Plural-s in die Lücken.*

Maggy is on a school exchange visit in England. Her suitcase........ have not arrived so far. She is very upset. Agnes, her English host sister, offers Maggy some of her own clothe........ Agnes........ clothe........ are quite trendy and Maggy likes them. Yesterday they went to Madame Susanne......., a new hairstyling salon in London. Agnes........and Maggy........ hair is now pink and very spiky. Maggy.....

mother saw it on Skype and could not stop laughing. She kept saying: "Oh my God!"

3. *Sage auf Englisch, dass …*

a) du jetzt zum Arzt gehst.

....

b) die letzten Ferien von Onkel Terry und Tante Joy furchtbar waren.

....

Test

3

1. *Entscheide welche Antwort stimmt.*

a) I am not feeling well. Let's go to
☐ the doctor's. ☐ doctors.

b) ☐ "Car's" ☐ "Cars" is the name of a kids movie.

c) It's raining ☐ cat and dog's ☐ cats and dogs.

d) ☐ Becky and James' ☐ Becky's and James's holidays were really good.

2. *Sage auf Englisch, dass …*

a) Anna bei ihren Großeltern ist.

....

b) Williams und Harolds Soldaten eine furchtbare Schlacht kämpften.

....

c) Louis Schwert sehr alt war.

....

Nomen

1

much, many/a lot of/some, any

Im Englischen unterscheidest du zählbare Nomen (5 Stück Kuchen, 2 Gläser) von nicht zählbaren Nomen (Mehl, Wasser). Bei den zählbaren verwendet man **many** als Mengenangabe **viel**, bei den nicht zählbaren **much**.

zählbare Nomen: many toys, many children, many apples

nicht zählbare Nomen: much water, much rain, much noise

Du verwendest **much** und **many** vor allem in Fragen und Verneinungen.

How much money is left? Not much.

How many apples have you got? Many!

Tipp:
Much kann auch **sehr** bedeuten, wenn es sich auf ein Verb bezieht: **I love my dog very much.**

Um Aussagesätze bilden zu können, verwendest du statt **much/many** oft **a lot of** oder **lots of**.

There is a lot of money in the bank.

Jessica has lots of clothes.

Achtung: Nach **as**, **so**, **too**, **how** und **very** kann man **much/many** nicht durch **a lot of** ersetzen.

2

1. *Sortiere die Wörter nach zählbaren und nicht zählbaren Nomen.*

milk, apples, cake, sugar, oranges, juice, eggs, fun, games, dolls, cars, music, songs, books, rain, sunshine, clouds, snowflakes, ice, umbrellas, frogs

zählbar	nicht zählbar

2. *Schreibe mit den Wörter aus Aufgabe 1 Sätze mit **much** oder **many**. Schreibe in den Heft.*

3. *Setze **much**, **many** oder **a lot of/lots** of ein.*

a) There isn't .... milk left, Sarah.

No, but we have .... apple juice.

b) How .... time do you need?

c) Oh, you have got so .... rabbits!

4. *Finde die Fehler und korrigiere den ganzen Satz.*

a) You have got much books!

....

b) I don't have so a lot of time.

....

c) You are allowed to make many noise.

....

Test

3

*Vervollständige die Sätze mit **much**, **many** und **a lot of** oder **lots of**.*

a) Thank you very ....

b) How .... doggy biscuits are left?

c) We have .... very nice girls in our class.

d) You have so .... nice flowers in your garden!

Nomen

1

some, any, no – Zusammensetzungen mit some und any

Um im Englischen **etwas**, **einige** oder **ein paar** ausdrücken zu können, musst du wissen, wie du **some** und **any** anwendest.

some – bejahte Aussagesätze und höfliche Fragen mit klarer Antwort.

There are some interesting places in London.
Could I have some more tea, please? Yes, of course.

any – Verneinungen und Fragen.

I don't have any questions.
Are there any children at the hotel?

Tipp:
In verneinten Sätzen kannst du **not + any** auch durch **no** ersetzen. Beides bedeutet **kein/keine**.

There isn't any cake left. There is no cake left.

2

1. *Some oder any? Kreuze an*

a) I would like	☐ some	☐ any	extra jam, please.
b) I don't have	☐ some	☐ any	French fries!
c) Are there	☐ some	☐ any	sweets left?

2. *Setze **some** oder **any** oder **no** richtig ein.*

a) Have you ever seen .... ghosts?

b) Yes, I saw .... when we went to Scotland last year.

c) Could you tell me .... stories about ghosts?

e) I think there are .... ghosts.

Tipp:
Die Zusammensetzungen mit **some** und **any** werden wie **some** und **any** verwendet (**something, somebody, someone, somewhere – anything, anybody, anyone, anywhere**).

3. *Finde die Fehler und schreibe den ganzen Satz richtig auf.*

a) Is there somebody out there?

....

b) I can see anything!

....

c) Could you do anything for me, please?

....

Test

3

Lies den Text und fülle die Lücken. Du brauchst nicht alle Wörter aus dem Wortvorrat.

some | any | anyone | anywhere | somewhere | somebody | something | anything | anybody | someone

Sherlock Holmes waited outside. "Can you see ...., Watson?" "No, I can't. It's too dark to see a person!" They waited. Suddenly they heard .... Was it the thief? They needed .... candles. Watson didn't have ...., but Sherlock Holmes found matches and a candle in his coat. "................................ must stop this thief!" said Watson, "Isn't there .... we can do?" "There is always .... who can do the right thing!" said Sherlock Holmes.

Nomen

1

Zählbare und nicht zählbare Nomen

Du kannst die zählbaren Nomen mit dem unbestimmten Artikel a und Zahlwörtern verbinden.

Is there a black dog? There are two black dogs.

Nicht zählbare Nomen können nicht direkt mit dem unbestimmten Artikel oder Zahlwörtern verbunden werden.

Wenn der bestimmte Artikel nicht ausreicht, benötigst du sogenannte Fügungen **(a piece of)**, die dir weiterhelfen. Diese kannst du mit Zahlwörtern verbinden.

two pieces of …

Nicht zählbare Nomen	Beispiele für geeignete Fügungen
milk, water, lemonade …	a bottle of …, a glass of …
tea, coffee	a cup of, a pot of …
chocolate	a piece of … a bar of
bread	a loaf of … a slice of
ice	a cube of ice, icecube

Sammelbegriffe wie **luggage** (Gepäck) oder **furniture** (Mobiliar, Möbel) sowie abstrakte Nomen wie **information**, **advice**, **progress**, **knowledge**, **homework** werden immer im Singular gebraucht.

furniture, luggage	a piece of
information, advice	a bit of …, a piece of …

Nomen, die auf -s enden und eine Einheit bezeichnen **(news, mathematics, The United States)** werden ebenfalls im Singular verwendet.

2

1. *Verbinde die Nomen mit den passenden Fügungen.*

a loaf of	information
a bottle of	chocolate
a piece of	coke
a bar of	bread

2. *Entscheide, ob der unbestimmte Artikel oder entsprechende Fügungen eingesetzt werden müssen.*

a) Do you have .... pen for me? –

No, but you can have .... pencil.

b) Would you like .... chocolate?

3. *Sage auf Englisch, dass ... Schreibe in dein Heft.*

a) dir dieses Möbelstück gut gefällt.
b) du drei Flaschen Wasser kaufen musst.

4. *Schreibe die Sätze korrigiert in dein Heft.*

a) Would you please give me a milk.
b) I need informations.
c) There is a tea waiting for you.

Test

3

1. *Am Flughafen. Fülle die Lücken im Dialog.*

Airline Staff: "Good morning, Sir. How many .... luggage are you checking in?" You: "Three. How many .... of water may I take with me?" Airline staff: "None. Sorry, Sir." You: "Oh. But I may take my .... chocolate, right?" Airline staff: "That is no problem, Sir."

2. *Sage auf Englisch, dass ... Schreibe in dein Heft.*

a) Anna einen Brief an ihre Austauschschülerin schreibt.
b) du einen Kaffee trinken möchtest.
c) Edmund niemals eine Cola trinken würde.

4. Pronomen

1

Personalpronomen und Possessivbegleiter

Auch im Englischen gibt es Personalpronomen (persönliche Fürworter). Diese können **Subjekt (Wer? Was?)** oder **Objekt (Wen? Wem?)** sein.

Peter is at home. He is asleep now. I want to visit him.

Um auszudrücken, wem etwas oder jemand gehört, verwendest du die Possessivbegleiter.

Subjekt	Wer? Was?
I	ich
you	du
he/she/it	er / sie/es
we	wir
you	ihr
they	sie (Mehrzahl!)

Objekt	Wen? Wem?
me	mir, mich
you	dir, dich
him/her/it	ihm, ihn/ihr, sie/ihm, es
us	uns
you	euch
them	ihnen, sie

Possessiv-begleiter	
my	mein
your	dein
his/her/its	sein/ihr/sein
our	unser
your	euer
their	ihr (Mehrzahl!)

2

1. *Ersetze das unterstrichene Subjekt des Satzes durch das korrekte Personalpronomen.*

a) Lucy is a nice girl.

b) The house is very big.

c) Paul and Pete are brothers.

d) John is never here.

2. *Setze das richtige Personalpronomen als Objekt ein.*

a) She gave it to .... (Sarah).

b) Give .... my glasses, please! (I)

c) We like .... (Katarina, Anna, Luka)

3. *Sieh dir die Wortpaare an und bilde Sätze mithilfe der Possessivbegleiter.*

a) James + cat This is .... cat.

b) I + shoes Where are ....?

c) Carla + skates These are .... skates.

d) Tom & Jerry This is .... problem.

4. *Sage auf Englisch, dass ...*

a) ihr früh (early) seid.

....

b) du aus Deutschland bist.

....

c) sie Fußball spielen.

....

Tipp:
it's (Kurz für **it is**) und **its** (Possessivbegleiter) solltest du nicht verwechseln. Du kannst den Unterschied nicht hören, sondern dir nur über den Inhalt des Satzes erschließen. Das gleiche gilt für **you're** (kurz für **you are**) und **your** (Possessivbegleiter) sowie **they're** (kurz für **they are**) und **their** (Possessivbegleiter).

Pronomen

5. *you're oder your, it's oder its, they're oder their? Kreuze an.*

a) Is this ☐ you're ☐ your bag?
b) ☐ It's ☐ its warm today.
c) ☐ Their ☐ They'r car is new.

6. *Richtig oder falsch? Kreuze an und korrigiere die falschen Sätze.*

	R	F
a) Can you see Rashid? I can't see him.	☐	☐
b) See your later!	☐	☐
c) Give him his book, please.	☐	☐
d) Can you help my?	☐	☐

....

....

....

....

7. *Lies den Text und setze die entsprechenden Personalpronomen und Possessivbegleiter ein.*

One day the young girl, Molly, wanted to go to town. .... father had told her not to go out alone. But .... was not at home, so Molly decided to go. .... put on .... best dress and left the house. It was a long way and Molly became tired. She went to sleep under a big tree. When .... woke up there was golden sand under .... feet and .... could hear lovely music. "Where am .... ?" And then she heard the most beautiful voice. .... whispered the secret message.

Test

1. *Setze das richtige Personalpronomen oder den richtigen Possessivbegleiter ein*

a) This is .... new dress. (Kate)

b) Just look at ....! She looks lovely.

c) Jason thinks .... looks lovely, too.

d) What do .... think, Finn?

2. *Sage auf Englisch, dass …*

a) unser Haus grün ist.

....

b) wir Schokoladeneis lieben.

....

c) ich keine Spinnen mag.

....

3. *Entscheide ob **you're** oder **your**, **it's** oder **its**, **they're** oder **their**.*

a) This is not .... (you're/your) problem!

b) I like .... (you're/your) new hairstyle.

c) .... (it's/its) very cold today!

d) The river is fast. .... water is very cold. (it's/its)

Pronomen

1

Possessivpronomen

Du hast die **Possessivbegleiter** in der 5. Klasse bereits kennengelernt. Die Possessivpronomen kannst du stellvertretend für ein Substantiv einsetzen. Sie können auch alleine stehen, das heißt sie **begleiten** ein Substantiv nicht, sondern sie ersetzen es.

This is my book. It's mine.

↑ ↑

Possessivbegleiter Possessivpronomen

mine	meins, das meine
yours	deins, das deine
his/hers/its	seines, ihres, seines
ours	unseres, das unsere
yours	eu[e]res, das eure
theirs	ihres, das ihre (Mehrzahl!)

Is this Sheila's pen? Yes, it is hers.
This is your new dog. Oh, it is mine!

Tipp:
Der Ausdruck „ein Freund von mir/dir/uns …" wird im Englischen auch mithilfe des Possessivpronomens gebildet.

Benjamin is a friend of mine.
Benjamin ist ein Freund von mir.

2

1. *Beantworte die Fragen.*

a) Oh, is that Nadja's notebook? Yes, that is ....

b) Is that my problem or Anna and Ben's problem?

No, it is ....

c) Hey, I know Andy, too. Is he a friend of ....?

2. *Übersetze ins Englisch. Schreibe in dein Heft.*

a) Ist das mein Platz? Ja, das ist deiner.

b) Ronja und Toni sind Freunde von ihnen.

c) Wessen (Whose) Bücher sind das? Das sind unsere.

3. *Vervollständige die Tabelle mit den entsprechenden Possessivpronomen und Possessivbegleitern.*

meins	mine		my
	yours	dein	
seins/ihrs/seins		sein/ihr/sein	
	ours		our
eu[e]res		euer	
ihres		ihr	

Test

3

1. *Finde die Fehler und schreibe den ganzen Satz korrigiert in dein Heft.*

a) Whose dirty socks are these? They are not my.

b) Theirs answers are very good.

c) The dog is huge. It's paws are as big as my hand!

2. *Sage auf Englisch, dass …*

a) Sheila und Anton Freunde von ihm sind.

....

b) dein Mantel hier ist, aber meiner nicht da ist.

....

Pronomen

1

Reflexivpronomen und each other

Reflexivpronomen verwendest du, wenn du ausdrücken willst, dass jemand etwas **für sich selbst** oder **auf sich bezogen** tut.

Ich kann mich selbst sehen.

Du kannst Reflexivpronomen auch verwenden, um besonders zu betonen.

Das hast du selbst getan (nicht jemand anderer).

myself	ich selbst, mir
yourself	dich selbst, dir, dich, sich
himself/herself/itself	sich/sich/sich
oneself	man selbst
ourselves	uns selbst, uns
yourselves	euch selbst, sich
themselves	sich (Mehrzahl!)

Folgende Verben werden im Englisch **nicht** reflexiv gebraucht:
sich verändern **(to change)**, sich beeilen **(to hurry)**,
sich bewegen **(to move)**, sich entscheiden **(to decide)**,
sich entspannen **(to relax)**, sich ereignen **(to happen)**,
sich erinnern **(to remember)**, sich fühlen **(to feel)**,
sich öffnen **(to open)**, sich treffen **(to meet)**

2

1. *Setze das passende Reflexivpronomen ein.*

a) I look at .... in the mirror.

b) Ben always thinks of .... first.

c) She has hurt ....

d) Let's take photos of ....

2. *Tom hat einen großen Fehler begangen.*
Setze das Reflexivpronomen ein, um zu betonen.

a) Tom, you knew .... that it was stupid to drive dad's new car.

b) You have created a big problem ....

c) Dad .... said that the repairs will be expensive!

d) I have never done something like that ....

Tipp:
Um auszudrücken, dass etwas „gegenseitig" geschieht, verwendest du **each other**.
They are looking at each other.

3. *Übersetze ins Englische. Entscheide, ob Reflexivpronomen nötig sind.*

a) Versuche, dich zu erinnern.

....

b) Hör dir selbst zu!

....

c) Ich fühle mich gut.

....

4. *Finde die Fehler und korrigiere den ganzen Satz.*

a) She never liked sheself.

....

Pronomen

b) They looked at each and laughed.

....

c) Try to remember yourself!

....

d) Grandmother himself told me the story.

....

5. *Sage auf Englisch, dass …*

a) wir uns gut fühlten.

....

b) es sich sehr langsam bewegte.

....

c) ich mir nicht wehtun soll.

....

6. *Vervollständige die Sätze.*

a) The forrest can't destroy ....

b) They were laughing about ....

c) I was shocked about ....

d) We have never locked .... out before.

d) Benjam and Franklin! Just look at ....

Test

3

*Lies den Text und entscheide, ob Reflexivpronomen nötig sind und welche – und wann du **each other** einsetzen kannst. Nicht jede Lücke muss gefüllt werden!*

Hello Rashid,

I must tell you what happened last week. My sister and I went camping on our own. I like to put the tent up ...., because Jill often makes a mess of it. She .... says that she is not good at it. Tsts, girls! Anyway, we were out in the wild, listening to .... sing and feeling .... good. Suddenly there was a really funny noise. Jill and I looked at .... We immediately thought: BEAR! The bears in Maine are not big, but you don't want to meet one .... We told .... to keep cool and I decided .... to have a look. I walked over to some bushes and then I found .... looking at some very long legs. I looked up and the owner of the legs looked down. We stared at .... for at least a minute before the moose (Elch) snorted, scratched .... and left. Boy, I was happy about meeting .... a moose and not a bear. How are your holidays? Have you had any adventures ....?

Yours Finn

5. Artikel

1

Der unbestimmte Artikel a, an – der bestimmte Artikel the

Bei Gegenständen oder Lebewesen verwendest du den unbestimmten Artikel a (ein, einer, eine) vor zählbaren Sustantiven. Wenn das nachfolgende Wort mit einem vokalischen Laut beginnt, hängst du ein -n an; aus dem unbestimmten Artikel a wird also an.

a bear, a comic, a shop
aber
an apple, an ice cream, an hour (das **h** spricht man nicht, daher muss man hier das **an** verwenden)

Der bestimmte Artikel lautet im Englischen immer the.
Es gibt eine Reihe Substantive, die in der Regel ohne **the** verwendet werden:

Tiergattungen	**Birds can fly.**
bestimmte Gruppe von Menschen	**Americans are friendly.**
Wochentage, Monate, (die meisten) Feiertage	**I love Christmas.** **Let's meet on Monday.**
Mahlzeiten	**Would you like to have lunch?**
öffentliche Einrichtungen	**London has many schools.**
Einzigartiges	**I love nature.**

2

1. *Setze a oder* ***an*** *ein.*

a) Could you pass me .... apple?

b) This is .... nice class.

c) We have to wait .... hour.

2. *Finde die Fehler und korrigiere den ganzen Satz. Schreibe in dein Heft.*

a) Yesterday I saw a elephant.
b) Today I want to see an monkey.

3. *Mit **the** oder ohne? Setze entsprechend ein.*

a) When does .... school begin in England?

b) .... family has dinner at eight.

c) We all like to go outside because we really

love .... nature.

d) Did you see .... tigers when you lived in India?

4. *Sage auf Englisch, dass …*

a) du jeden Tag zur Schule gehst.

....

b) du jeden Tag eine Banane isst.

....

c) du Pferde liebst.

....

5. *Richtig oder falsch? Kreuze an und korrigiere die falschen Sätze in deinem Heft.*

	R	F
a) Pass me a orange, please.	☐	☐
b) Where is the train station?	☐	☐
c) I don't like the Mondays.	☐	☐

Artikel

6. *Falls du **a** davorsetzen kannst, male die Kästchen blau an, falls du **an** einsetzen musst, male sie rot an. Trage die jeweiligen Artikel ein.*

a) ☐ .... old man

b) ☐ .... pretty girl

c) ☐ .... dangerous bus stop

d) ☐ .... interesting story

e) ☐ .... exciting holiday

7. *Bilde mit den Wortgruppen aus Aufgabe 6 ganze Sätze.*

a) ....

....

....

b) ....

....

....

c) ....

....

....

d) ....

....

....

e) ....

....

....

Test

1. *Setze **a**, **an** oder **the** ein. Achtung: manchmal brauchst du gar keinen Artikel!*

a) Do you like ....show?

b) I live in .... old house.

c) My grandparents have .... hens and .... goats.

d) Would you like to have .... dinner with me?

2. *Sage auf Englisch, dass…*

a) deine Klasse einen netten Lehrer hat.

....

b) Schüler gerne reden.

....

3. *Vervollständige die Sätze mit dem richtigen Artikel.*

a) She lives in .... very old house.

b) They live in .... old house, too.

c) I love .... nature.

d) Don't forget to take .... umbrella.

e) We can't see .... road!

6. Adjektive und Adverbien

1

Adjektiv oder Adverb?

Adjektive verwendest du, um Personen, Dinge oder Umstände zu beschreiben. Du drückst mit ihnen aus, **wie jemand oder etwas ist**.

a beautiful garden
a sunny day
a pretty girl

Adverbien helfen dir zu beschreiben, **wie jemand etwas tut**; sie beschreiben die Tätigkeit und beziehen sich somit immer auf das Verb. Du bildest die meisten Adverbien, indem du ein **-ly** an das Adjektiv anhängst.

She sings beautifully.
He hides quickly.

Adverbien der Art und Weise:	**Wie macht** man etwas?
Adjektiv:	**Wie ist** etwas?

Es gibt bei der Bildung von Adverbien folgende Ausnahmen und unregelmäßige Formen:

-y wird zu -i: angry → angrily happy → happily
-le wird zu -ly: terrible → terribly horrible → horribly
nach -ic wird ein -ally angehängt: fantastic → fantastically

Unregelmäßig gebildete Adverbien sind:
good → well; fast → fast; hard → hard

2

1. *Bilde die Adverbien aus diesen Wörtern.*

a) nice ....
b) loud ....
c) good ....
d) new ....
e) bad ....
f) awful ....

2. *Richtig oder falsch? Kreuze an und korrigiere, wenn nötig.*

	R	F
a) She called out loud.	☐	☐
....		
b) Please walk slowly!	☐	☐
....		
c) That was good done!	☐	☐
....		

3. *Adverb oder Adjektiv? Setze entsprechend ein.*

a) I am a .... good/well tennis player.

b) Lynn can sing .... beautiful/beautifully.

c) We work very .... hard/hardly.

d) Please carry the bowl .... careful/carefully.

4. *Sage auf Englisch, dass …*

a) Benjamin schön singt.

....

b) du gut Haare schneiden kannst.

....

5. *Finde die Fehler und korrigiere den ganzen Satz.*

a) The baby cries loud.

....

b) The dog is happily.

....

Adjektive und Adverbien

Tipp:
Adjektive und Adverbien können bei Verben des Geruchs oder des Geschmacks stehen. Sie können in diesem Zusammenhang aber nicht beliebig verwendet werden, es ändert sich nämlich jeweils die Bedeutung des Satzes!
Beispielsätze können dies verdeutlichen:

The cake tastes good. (Der Kuchen schmeckt gut)
Jamie Oliver tastes well. (Jamie Oliver kann gut verkosten/schmecken.)

Für **good/well** gilt außerdem:

Anna looks good. (Linda sieht gut/hübsch aus.)
Linda looks well. (Linda sieht fit/gesund aus. → Sie war vielleicht krank und sieht jetzt wieder fit aus.)

Lerne diese Beispielsätze am besten auswendig und merke Dir die Situation, in denen du sie verwenden kannst.

6. *Setze die richtigen Adjektive und Adverbien ein.*

perfectly | beautiful | happy | well | fantastic | happily | old

This is Anna's family. Her sister Leni is 18 years old and she is very .... Leni can dance very ....
Mina is the middle sister. She loves to cook and she can taste very .... She wants to have her own restaurant and create her own food. Her cakes are always ....
Anna's parents love dogs, so the family has a dog, Nelly.
Nelly is a very .... dog. When Anna throws a ball she runs after it .... They all live in an .... house.

7. *Übersetze.*

a) Linda hat ein neues Kleid. Es sieht gut aus.

....

b) Ich kann sehr gut riechen.

....

c) Der Pullover riecht nicht gut.

....

8. *Vervollständige die Regel.*

Adjektive beschreiben,

....

....

Adverbien beschreiben,

....

....

9. *Setze die fehlenden Adverbien ein.*

a) Jamie Oliver is a good cook.

He cooks ....

b) Anna is a fast learner.

She always learns ....

10. *Übersetze diese Fragen.*

a) Singt der Vogel laut? ....

....

Adjektive und Adverbien

b) Kannst Du deine Vokabeln bitte leise üben? ....

....

c) Schmeckt die Pizza gut? ....

....

11. *Setze die richtigen Adverbien oder Adjektive ein.*

nervously | happy | wonderful | lovingly | sad | best | prettily

We were very .... The Christmas holiday had started and we were on our way home. Only Jane felt .... "Is the new house nice?" she asked .... "I really liked our old house. I don't want to live in a new house." she told me. I put my arm around her .... and gave her my .... smile.

"It is ...., Jane. From your room you can see the sea and the beach." Her parents had decorated her room .... with seashells and little boats.

12. *Finde die Fehler und korrigiere den ganzen Satz in deinem Heft.*

a) They laughed nervous.
b) You have a loudly voice.
c) The never do things nice.

Test

1. *Richtig oder falsch? Streiche das falsche Wort durch und schreibe den ganzen Satz richtig in dein Heft.*

a) John sings **beautiful/beautifully**.

b) Anna was very ill. Today she looks **good/well**.

c) He listens **carful/carefully**.

d) That birthday party was **good/well**.

2. *Setze die fehlenden Adverbien ein.*

a) Our teacher is nice.

She always treats us ....

b) Kevin is a slow writer.

He writes ....

3. *Sage auf Englisch, dass ...*

a) Ben hart arbeitet.

....

b) du ein guter Fußballspieler bist.

....

c) dein Vater gut kochen kann.

....

d) deine Freundin gut aussieht.

....

Adjektive und Adverbien

1

Steigerung der Adjektive

Die Steigerungsformen der Adjektive und Adverbien sind vor allem geeignet, zu vergleichen.

he is older ...; he is as old as ...

Für einsilbige Adjektive und Adverbien und zweisilbige, die auf -y enden, wird die Steigerung mit -er und -est gebildet.

old	older	oldest
cool	cooler	coolest
happy	happier	happiest
pretty	prettier	prettiest

Zwei- und mehrsilbige Adjektive und Adverbien werden gesteigert, indem man more und most verwendet.

beautiful	more beautiful	most beautiful
interesting	more interesting	most interesting

Unregelmäßige Formen sind:

good	better	best
beautiful	more beautiful	most beautiful
well	better	best
much	more	most
many	more	most
little	less	least

2

1. *Steigere diese Adjektive und Adverbien.*

a) high ....

b) big ....

c) little ....

d) terrible ....

e) bad ....

2. *Steigere diese Aussagen.*

a) Lynn sings beautifully. Yes, but Anna sings ....

But Ronja sings ....

b) Toni runs fast. Ben runs .... But Dave runs ....

c) That was bad news. This is .... news. Let's hope there

will not be the .... news.

3. *Vervollständige die Tabelle mit den entsprechenden Steigerungsformen.*

terrible		
good		
nice		
clear		
little		
slow		

4. *Sage auf Englisch, dass…*

a) dein Test besser ist.

....

b) das die beste Party war.

....

c) Luka am meisten Geschenke bekommen hat.

....

Adjektive und Adverbien

5. *Setze die korrekte Form der Steigerung ein.*

a) James is the .... (fast) runner at our school.

b) Jenny is a .... (good) dancer than Betty.

c) Ann was a .... (famous) queen, but Elizabeth the first was the .... (famous) queen of England.

d) Archibald is the .... (big) dog I have ever seen!

6. *Finde die Fehler und schreibe den ganzen Satz.*

a) A mouse is smaler than a rat.

....

b) That was the dangeroust thing I have ever done.

....

c) Being thirsty is badder than being hungry.

....

7. *Frage auf Englisch, ob …*

a) der Kuchen süßer ist als das Eis.

....

b) die Königin schöner ist als die Prinzessin.

....

c) der Elefant das stärkste Tier ist.

....

Test

1. *Sage auf Englisch, dass …*

a) „The never ending story“ ein wundervolles Buch ist.

....

....

b) das Experiment interessanter ist als der Text.

....

c) du das beste Eis der Stadt gegessen hast.

....

2. *Finde die Fehler und schreibe den Satz richtig auf.*

a) I had the badest dream!

....

b) Who is the most nicest girl?

....

c) That dog is more small than my cat.

....

3. *Setze richtig ein.*

a) Your English is not .... (schlecht).

b) They have the .... (beste) pizza in town.

Adjektive und Adverbien

1

Vergleiche mit Adjektiven as ... as, ... than ...

Um Gleichheit auszudrücken, verwendest du as ... as (so ... wie).

Anna runs as fast as Mina. It is as good as new.

Um Ungleichheit auszudrücken, hast du zwei Möglichkeiten:

1. **not as ... as** (nicht so ... wie)
   not as good as
2. Komparativ + than
   higher than, nicer than

Tipp:
Eselsbrücke, um **than** und **then** nicht zu verwechseln:
bigger than –größer als ... also immer mit a.

2

1. *Vergleiche und schreibe den ganzen Satz.*

a) mountain/hill + high

....

b) river/stream (Bach) + wide

....

c) pony/horse + small

....

2. *Drücke die Gemeinsamkeiten zwischen Lynn und Leni aus.*

a) Lynn/Leni + tall

....

b) Lynn's hair/Leni's hair + long

....

c) Lynn's voice/Leni's voice + strong

....

d) Lynn/Leni + talk much

....

3. *Übersetze ins Englische und setze an der richtigen Stelle ein.*

nicht so heiß wie | so teuer wie | schwieriger als

a) A smartphone is .... a camera.

b) Chinese is .... English.

c) Germany is .... Australia.

4. *Sage auf Englisch, dass ...*

a) du schneller rennst als dein Freund.

....

b) deine Mutter so gut kocht wie dein Vater.

....

c) dein Englisch besser ist als dein Französisch.

....

5. *Markiere die Fehler farbig und korrigiere den ganzen Satz.*

a) This is worse then I thought.

....

b) My present is as big than yours.

....

Adjektive und Adverbien

6. *Drücke die Unterschiede zwischen Sam und Stan in zwei Sätzen aus.*

a) Sam: tall Stan: not as tall

....

....

b) Sam: good at Math Stan: not as good at Math

....

....

c) Sam: good dancer Stan: better dancer

....

....

7. *Frage auf Englisch, ob …*

a) ich besser koche als singe.

....

b) meine Ferien länger sind als deine.

....

c) der Film so gut ist wie das Buch.

....

8. *Vervollständige den Text.*

Dear Grandma,

We have finally arrived in Arizona. The countryside is

.... interesting .... you can imagine!

The weather here is awesome – although it is not

.... hot .... I thought. Many people run around wearing real cowboy hats which I find very cool. They are much cooler .... the people at home. I'll write again soon and send a picture with me and my new hat!

Yours Dylan

Test

3

1. *Finde den Fehler und schreibe den Satz korrigiert auf.*

a) This holiday was better then the last.

....

b) Megan is as sad Tom.

....

c) Sunday is not as bad than Monday.

....

2. *Vergleiche und formuliere ganze Sätze.*

a) that film / this film + good (Gleichheit)

....

b) this song / that song + better (Ungleichheit)

....

a) this book/ that book + interesting (Ungleichheit)

....

b) this hobby/ that hobby + dangerous (Gleichheit)

....

7. Adverbien

1

Häufigkeitsadverbien und Stellung im Satz

Die Häufigkeitsadverbien in Englisch sind:
always, usually, regularly, normally, often, sometimes, occasionally, rarely, seldom, never.

Normalerweise stehen diese Verben direkt vor dem Vollverb.

I always go for a walk.

Die Häufigkeitsadverbien stehen allerdings nach einer Form von to be **(am, is, are, was, were)**.

I am never late.

Often, usually, sometimes können auch am Satzanfang oder am Satzende stehen.

Sometimes I watch the sunrise.
We go to Munich occasionally.

2

1. *Finde die Fehler und korrigiere den ganzen Satz.*

a) Always you are dreaming.

....

b) We go often swimming.

....

c) Becky is late always.

....

d) Max shouts never.

....

2. *Setze die Adverbien an die richtige Stelle im Satz.*

a) Anna is very friendly (usually).

....

b) I go for a walk (always).

....

c) My dog barks (sometimes).

....

d) Do you jog (often)?

....

3. *Sage auf Englisch, dass …*

a) du deine Großmutter regelmäßig besuchst.

....

b) wir selten Hausaufgaben am Freitag bekommen.

....

c) Layla sich oft langweilt.

....

4. *Vervollständige die Regel.*

Häufigkeitsadverbien stehen ....

.... Wenn aber eine Form von ....

im Satz steht, so stehen die Häufigkeitsadverbien ....

....

Adverbien

5. *Finde die Häufigkeitsadverbien in diesem Raster und markiere sie farbig.*

Q	W	E	R	T	Z	U	I	O
S	A	L	W	A	Y	S	P	F
R	I	P	L	C	Y	U	L	T
N	E	V	E	R	A	A	K	E
T	Y	V	M	V	S	L	H	N
N	N	O	R	M	A	L	L	Y
T	M	R	N	B	D	Y	G	F
S	O	M	E	T	I	M	E	S

6. *Bilde aus diesen Bausteinen Sätze.*

a) never I come late home

....

b) we to regularly the go theatre

....

c) often she doesn't her visit grandmother

....

d) don't you late sleep normally

....

7. *Welches Wort passt nicht in die Gruppe? Streiche es durch*

a) often/regularly/normally/never

b) seldom/occasionally/sometimes/usually

Test

1. *Sage auf Englisch, dass …*

a) dein Bruder sich selten aufregt.

....

b) sie normalerweise spät aufstehen.

....

c) du oft Radio hörst.

....

2. *Platziere die Häufigkeitsadverbien an der richtigen Stelle.*

a) My father takes milk in his tea (sometimes).

....

b) I do my homework (usually).

....

c) We go to the gym (regularly).

....

3. *Streiche das nicht passende Wort.*

a) I **sometimes/never** go to the gym, but I should go more often.
b) Do you visit your cousin in the States **regularly/usually**?
c) They are **always/occasionally** late. It drives me crazy!

Adverbien

1 Adverbiale Bestimmung und Stellung im Satz

Was		Stellung im Satz	Beispiel
Satz-adverbien	of course, maybe, suddenly, unfortunately, then, at first	vor dem Subjekt	Maybe the teacher is late.
Modal-adverbien	carefully, well, badly, quickly	nach Vollverb oder Objekt	Her mood changed quickly.
Temporal-adverbien	today, tomorrow, yesterday, then, …	nach Vollverb oder Objekt	School starts next week.
Lokal-adverbien	here, there, in, to, at …	nach Vollverb oder Objekt	My father lives in New York.
Grad-adverbien	very, quite, nearly, too, fairly, really, hardly	direkt vor dem Verb, welches verstärkt oder abgeschwächt wird.	Megan was quite scared.

Tipp:
Einige Verben beschreiben keine Tätigkeiten sondern **Zustände oder Eigenschaften**, die sogenannten **„Zustandsverben“**.

Nach diesen Verben steht meist ein Adjektiv:
be, become, feel, get, seem, sound.

I am tired.
She became hungry.
He felt bad.
It got cold.
We seemed lost.
This sounds good.

2

1. *Platziere die adverbiale Bestimmung an der richtigen Stelle.*

a) Zoe goes to see movies at the weekend. (always)

....

b) She comes home on time. (never)

....

c) Her mother is upset. (of course)

....

d) Zoe is tired because she sleeps enough. (hardly)

....

2. *Sage auf Englisch, dass …*

a) du normalerweise samstags deine Freunde triffst.

....

b) diese Idee gut klingt.

....

c) du plötzlich furchtbare Kopfschmerzen hattest.

....

d) sie fast einen Unfall gehabt hätte.

....

3. *Finde die Fehler und schreibe den ganzen Satz korrigiert in dein Heft.*

a) James doesn't play well football.
b) The children became hungrily.
c) That was dangerous quite!
d) I unfortunately can't come.

Adverbien

4. *Entscheide, ob du das Adjektive oder das Adverb einsetzen musst. Streiche das falsche Wort.*

a) Why are you always **late/lately**, Zoe?

b) What is so **terrible/terribly** about being late, Mum?

c) She does her work **careful/carefully**.

d) This pizza smells **good/well**!

5. *Schreibe den Satz mithilfe des Verbs in Klammer und der adverbialen Bestimmungen um, ohne die Bedeutung zu verändern.*

a) Most sportsmen are fair players. (to play)

....

b) Anna makes lovely cakes. (to bake)

....

c) Luka is a good driver. (to drive)

....

d) I am a fast reader. (to read)

....

6. *Unterstreiche die adverbialen Bestimmungen in diesem Text.*

For many people London is one the most exciting cities. People from all over the world come to see its fascinating historic sights. It's hardly possible to see everything in one visit. There are nearly 5000 overseas banks in the financial centre of the city, so London is an important European business centre.

Test

1. *Sage auf Englisch, dass …*

a) du gut riechen kannst.

....

b) sich das Wetter hier schnell ändert.

....

c) du dich krank fühlst.

....

2. *Finde den Fehler und schreibe den ganzen Satz in dein Heft.*

a) Never I will see you again!

b) The keys here are!

c) We can maybe wait and see?

3. *Adjektiv oder Adverb?*

a) She walks around ☐ slow ☐ slowly.

b) He is very ☐ careful ☐ carefully.

4. *Schreibe die Sätze mithilfe adverbialer Bestimmungen um, ohne die Bedeutung zu verändern.*

a) Life is often a surprise. (to surprise)

....

b) His photographs are very good. (to take pictures)

....

c) Zoe is a bad liar. (to lie)

....

8. Satzbau

1

Aussagesatz, Imperativ, Fragesatz

Merke dir die Abkürzung SVOPT für den Satzbau der Aussagesätze im Englischen.

Subjekt (subject) S	Prädikat (verb) V	Objekt (object) O	Ort (place) P	Zeit (time) T
She	reads	the newspaper	in her room	every morning
wer	was	mit wem/was	wo	wann

Du verwendest den Imperativ um **Befehle, Aufforderungen, Bitten** und **Verbote** auszudrücken. Dabei wird nicht zwischen Singular und Plural unterschieden, die Form bleibt immer gleich, unabhängig davon, wie viele Personen angesprochen werden.

positiv	Come here. Look.
negativ	Don't do that. Don't look.

Der Satzbau in Fragesätzen **mit Vollverb** sieht so aus:

Fragewort	do/does (simple present) did (simple past)	Subjekt	Verb
What	do	you	think?
Where	did	she	live?

Der Satzbau in Fragesätzen sieht so aus:

Fragewort	Hilfsverb	Subjekt	Verb
What	is	he	doing?
Where	has	she	gone?

1. *Finde die Fehler und korrigiere den ganzen Satz.*

a) My family in an old house lives.

....

b) You are where?

....

c) We pizza eat every weekend.

....

2. *Bilde Aussagesätze aus diesen Wörtern. Beachte die Zeitangabe.*

a) listen to / radio / she / every morning

....

b) at night / they / share / secrets

....

c) visit / his grandparents / he / every day

....

3. *Bilde Fragesätze aus diesen Wörtern.*

a) you / what / eat / in the morning

....

b) she / where / does / live

....

c) the / new girl / is / who

....

Satzbau

4. *Sage auf Englisch, dass …*

a) dein Vater im Garten ist.

....

b) dein Vater jeden Morgen die Zeitung liest.

....

c) dein Vater jeden Abend die Nachrichten sieht.

....

5. *Vervollständige die Regel.*

Aussagesätze

Der Satzbau in Aussagesätzen sieht so aus:

....

....

....

Fragesätze mit Vollverb

Bei Fragesätzen mit Vollverb

....

....

....

Fragesätze mit Hilfsverb

Ist ein Hilfsverb im Satz, sieht der Satzbau so aus:

....

....

....

6. *Bilde Sätze.*

a) I/at the moment/doing my homework/am

....

b) the window/open

....

c) never/that/do

....

Test

3

1. *Bringe den Wortsalat in die richtige Reihenfolge.*

a) smell | the flowers | lovely | in the afternoon

....

b) looks | very scary | the old house | at night

....

c) in the morning | feel | I | sleepy

....

2. *Übersetze.*

a) Ich wohne in einer kleinen Stadt in Deutschland.

....

b) Wir wollen heute morgen schwimmen gehen.

....

c) Der Hund läuft jeden Abend die Straße hinunter.

....

9. If-Sätze

1

If-Satz Typ 1: Wahrscheinlichkeit

Um im Englischen Bedingungen auszudrücken, verwendest du die sogenannten If-Sätze. Der **If-Satz Typ 1 drückt aus, dass etwas wahrscheinlich ist**. Der If-Satz besteht aus zwei Teilen: einem **Hauptsatz (main clause)** und einem **Nebensatz (if-clause)**. Die Reihenfolge dieser beiden Teilsätze kann vertauscht werden. Im main clause verwendest du das will-future, im if-clause das simple present.

main clause ↓	if-clause ↓
I will go to the beach	if the sun shines.
If the sun shines,	I will go to the beach.
↑ if-clause	↑ main clause

Das **Komma** wird nur in der Variante if-clause **vor** main clause verwendet.

Bei der Verneinung musst du überlegen, welchen Teil du verneinen willst.

main clause ↓	if-clause ↓
I will not go to the beach	if it rains.
I will go to the beach	if it doesn't rain.

Tipp:
If kann mit **falls** übersetzt werden. **When** bezieht sich auf den Zeitpunkt, an dem etwas geschehen wird, und kann mit **sobald** übersetzt werden. When-Sätze werden wie If-Sätze gebildet.

1. *Finde die Fehler und korrigiere den ganzen Satz.*

a) If you will call me, I tell you the story.

....

b) She buys the dress if she has enough money.

....

c) We will not come if you will not ask us.

....

2. *If oder when? Kreuze an.*

a) ☐ If ☐ When we have the new car, we will go for a drive.

b) ☐ If ☐ When you are late again, mum will be angry!

3. *Sage auf Englisch, dass … (achte auf **if** und **when**)*

a) du nicht zur Party darfst, wenn du dein Zimmer nicht aufräumst.

....

b) deine Familie nach Paris fliegt, wenn deine Tante Geburtstag hat.

....

c) Ben glücklich sein wird, wenn Anna wirklich anruft.

....

4. *Bilde If-Sätze aus diesen Satzblöcken.*

a) not do my homework/ not go out

....

b) use less salt/ food taste better

....

If-Sätze

5. *Vervollständige die Sätze.*

a) My brother .... (miss) the train

if he doesn't hurry.

b) My sister .... (buy) the red shoes

if she has enough money.

c) If my father .... (like) the black

jeep, he .... (buy) it.

d) If my mother .... (finish) her Italian

class, she .... (travel) to Italy.

6. *Vervollständige die Sätze, indem du If-satz und den Hauptsatz verbindest. Schreibe die kompletten Sätze.*

If-Satz + Hauptsatz

a) Sam (to help) David + they (to go) to the beach

b) you (to go) to bed so late + I (to get) wet

c) a lion (to be) hungry + he (to hunt) for food

d) the pupils (to have) enough time + they (to finish) the test

e) it (to snow) + I (to build) a snowman

a) ....

....

b) ....

....

c) ....

....

d) ....

....

e) ....

....

Test

3

1. *Sage auf Englisch, dass …*

a) du den Bus noch bekommst, wenn du dich beeilst.

....

b) Anna mit Tom essen geht, wenn er sie fragt.

....

2. *Finde den Fehler und korrigiere den ganzen Satz.*

a) They won't be quiet if there will be so much noise outside.

....

b) He wins the match if he plays like this.

....

3. *Bilde If-Sätze oder When-Sätze aus den Satzblöcken.*

a) to be 18 | I learn to drive

....

b) Tom buy a house in Spain | earn a lot of money

....

If-Sätze

1

If-Satz Typ 2 und Typ 3: unwahrscheinlich und unmöglich

Der If-Satz Typ 2 drückt aus, dass etwas **unwahrscheinlich** ist.
Der If-Satz Typ 3 drückt aus, dass etwas **unmöglich** ist (weil es schon passiert ist).

If-Satz Typ 2	**if-clause:** simple past If I knew,	**main clause:** would + Grundform I would tell you.
If-Satz Typ 3	**if-clause:** past perfect If I had known,	**main clause:** would + have + III Form I would have told you.

2

1. *Bilde If-Sätze Typ 2, indem du die passenden Satzteile verbindest. Schreibe die vollständigen Sätze auf.*

… the cat (to cross) the road …	… we (to save) the planet.
… we (to run) fast enough …	… we (to catch) the bus.
… all of us (to help) …	… it (to be) in great danger.

....

....

....

....

2. *Vervollständige die Sätze.*

a) My test .... (to be better) if I .... (to study more).

b) You .... (not be so tired) if you .... (to go to bed earlier).

c) If he .... (to have her mobile number), he .... (to call her).

3. *Vervollständige den Text, indem du die richtige Verbform für die Bedingungssätze Typ 1, 2 und 3 wählst.*

Have you ever been to the rainforest? The biggest rainforest is in Brazil. It is on the Amazon river and you have probably heard about it. It is in great danger. If we .... (not/stop) to cut down the forest, there .... (not/be) any rainforest left in 100 years. But why do people of big companies do that? They want more grazing land for their cows so they can sell more meat to fast food restaurants or meat factories. But if the rainforest .... (to disappear/ verschwinden), millions of animals .... (to die). If we .... (to burn) more trees there every day, the weather .... (to change) and it .... (to get) warmer. If there .... (to be) no more rainforest to filter the air, it .... (not/be) clean anymore.

4. *Sage auf Englisch, dass …*

a) dein Test besser gewesen wäre wenn du mehr gelernt hättest.

....

....

b) dein Freund sich wehtun wird, wenn er so schnell fährt.

....

....

If-Sätze

c) du nicht so nass geworden wärst, wenn du einen Schirm mitgenommen hättest. ....

....

d) es nicht so schlimm wäre, wenn es nicht so wehtun würde.

....

....

5. *Welcher Typ Bedingungssatz ist das?*

a) If she had known about this, she would not have married him.

Typ ....

b) They would escape if they were cleverer.

Typ ....

c) We would have gone to the cinema if it hadn't been so expensive.

Typ ....

6. *Finde die Fehler und schreibe den ganzen Satz korrigiert.*

a) If it had never happened, they will be happy.

....

....

b) She wouldn't have this problem if she has been faster.

....

....

3

Test

1. *Sage auf Englisch, dass…*

a) du die Tür öffnen würdest, hättest Du deine Schlüssel nicht verloren.

....

....

b) dein Bruder nicht pünktlich sein würde, wenn er jetzt nicht gegangen wäre.

....

....

c) dein Lehrer die Tests schneller korrigieren würde, wenn er mehr Zeit hätte.

....

....

2. *Vervollständige die Sätze.*

a) If we .... (to know), we .... (to help) you.

b) I .... (go) to the concert if .... (to have) the money for the ticket.

c) If he .... (not eat) so much cake at the party, he .... (to feel) sick later.

10. Relativsätze

1

Relativsätze mit und ohne Relativpronomen

Um eine Person oder eine Sache genauer zu beschreiben, kannst du einen Relativsatz (relative clause) verwenden. Dazu benötigst du meist Relativpronomen.

who	der, die, das	bezieht sich auf Personen
which	das	bezieht sich auf Tiere oder Dinge
that	der, die, das	kann sich auf Personen, Tiere oder Dinge beziehen

Hauptsatz Relativsatz

Becky is the girl **who** likes dogs.
S V O

I use a computer which is quite old.
This is the car that was stolen last week.

Der **Satzbau** im Relativsatz ist wie im Hauptsatz (**S**ubjekt – **V**erb – **O**bjekt), und du benötigst zwischen Hauptsatz und Relativsatz **kein Komma**, wenn der Relativsatz notwendig ist, um die Person oder die Sache zu „definieren" **(defining relative clause)**. Wenn es sich aber nur um Zusatzinformationen handelt, also solche, die gesagt werden können aber nicht müssen, dann steht ein Komma vor und eins nach dem Relativsatz **(non-defining relative clause)**.

Her new dress, which everybody loves, is red.

Wenn das Relativpronomen sich auf das Objekt des Satzes bezieht, kannst du es auch weglassen. Aus dem **relative clause** wird so ein **contact clause**.

This is boy who we saw yesterday
→ This is the boy we saw yesterday.

2

1. *Unterstreiche den Relativsatz und markiere das Relativpronomen.*

a) This is the program about the rainforest which I saw yesterday.
b) There was a man who lives in the rainforest.
c) He lives there with the Kayapo, who are an Indian tribe.

2. *Füge das richtige Relativpronomen ein.*

a) Benjamin is a boy .... loves sports.

b) Anna. "This is the hairstyle .... I want to have."

c) Where are the people .... asked for me?

3. *Unterstreiche den Hauptsatz orange und den Relativsatz blau.*

a) Can you see the tiger which is jumping over the burning fence?
b) My favorite book is a fairytale book that my mum always read to me.
c) All the students who forgot their homework have to come to the front.

4. *Setzte die Kommas, wo sie nötig sind. Unterscheide zwischen defining und non-defining relative clause.*

a) This book which I love is about a big adventure.
b) There is the bus which I just missed.
c) I have a music CD which is really good.

5. *Finde die Fehler und korrigiere den ganzen Satz.*

a) Do you know the girl which is standing in the corner?

....

b) The dogs who look like lions are my favourite.

....

c) Where is the boy which broke his arm last week?

....

Relativsätze

Tipp:
Um zu kontrollieren, ob du das Relativpronomen weglassen kannst oder nicht, stell die Subjekt- oder Objektfrage:
Subjekt: wer oder was? (es muss stehen bleiben)
Objekt: wen oder was/wem? (es kann wegfallen)

6. *Kannst du hier das Relativpronomen weglassen? Kreuze an.*

	mit	ohne
a) This is a frog which is very toxic (giftig).	☐	☐
b) This is the window that I cleaned yesterday.	☐	☐
c) A Kapayo is a person who lives in the rainforest.	☐	☐
d) This was the TV program which I saw yesterday.	☐	☐

7. *Finde den Fehler und korrigieren den ganzen Satz.*

a) Many years ago, I went to the rainforest who is on the Amazonas.

....

....

b) There were many plants taht I had never seen before.

....

c) There were also some animals witch looked very strange.

....

8. *Übersetze. Entscheide, ob du das Relativpronomen weglassen kannst.*

a) Das ist das Mädchen, das so eine schöne Stimme (voice) hat.

....

....

b) Ich mag den Film, den ich gestern gesehen habe.

....

....

c) Wer kennt das Lied, das vom Regenwald handelt?

....

....

d) Hast du das Geschenk, das ich für dich gekauft habe?

....

....

9. *Wird das Relativpronomen in diesen Sätzen als Subjekt oder als Objekt verwendet?*
Streiche es durch, falls man es weglassen kann und schreibe die Sätze neu.

a) Anna started a campaign that helps to protect the rainforest.

....

....

b) The red-eyed frog is in the book which I bought last week.

....

....

c) The meat that the fast food restaurants sell is part of the problem. ....

....

Relativsätze

10. *Verbinde die beiden Sätze zu einem Satz.*
*Beginne jeden Satz mit **The**.*

A man has gone to prison. He stole a painting.

The man who stole the painting has gone to prison.

a) A scientist has won the Nobel Prize. He discovered a new planet.

....

....

b) A student had to leave school. He took drugs.

....

....

c) A little girl has been found. She had been lost in a National Park.

....

....

11. *Vervollständige die Sätze.*

a) The girl .... paid for the ice cream is Mary's friend.

b) From here you can see the mountain .... we climbed.

c) The detective lost the man .... he was following.

d) The pony .... I used to ride is very old now.

Test

3

1. *Vervollständige die Sätze.*

a) Basketball is a game … (to be fast)

....

b) Mrs Little is the teacher … (to teach maths)

....

c) France is a country … (to be famous for food and wine)

....

....

2. *Füge das passende Relativpronomen ein und verbinde die beiden Sätze zu einem Satz.*

a) This is my grandmother Iris. She lives in India.

....

b) India is a big country. It fascinates many people.

....

c) There are many interesting places. They are beautiful.

....

3. *Setze die Kommas, wo nötig.*

a) The rainforest tribes are people who live in the rainforest.

b) To protect the rainforest area which they live in is a very important goal.

Relativsätze

1

Freie Relativsätze

Freie Relativsätze können **allein stehen und beschreiben kein Subjekt oder Objekt näher**. Sie können vielmehr selbst Subjekt oder Objekt des Satzes sein. Hier verwendet man oft **where, what, when** und manchmal **who**. Häufig sind auch **whatever, whenever, wherever, whoever**.

She loves what she is. He has what we want.

Falls das Verb in einem contact clause eine Präposition hat (interested in, look at, listen to), dann stellst du diese an das Ende des contact clause.

This is the CD we are listening to.

2

1. *Sage auf Englisch, dass ...*

a) du mitbringst, was auch immer deine Familie braucht.

....

b) es nicht da war, wo es sein sollte.

....

2. *Setze das passende Relativpronomen ein.*

a) I can leave .... you you are ready.

b) .... made me nervous was their idea of having fun.

3. *Setze die Präposition **to** an die richtige Stelle.*

a) Most of the songs .... which .... we .... listened .... were .... very good.

b) This is the decision .... that .... we .... came ....

4. *Unterstreiche das Relativpronomen und entscheide, ob es ein freier Relativsatz ist oder nicht.*

a) I need an idea that will save me. Freier Relativsatz ☐

b) They did what they wanted. Freier Relativsatz ☐

Test

3

1. *Sage auf Englisch, dass …*

a) wer auch immer Anna die Blumen geschickt hat, sie zum Lächeln gebracht hat.

....

....

b) Anna liebt, was sie hört.

....

c) sie ging wo auch immer der Wind sie hintrug.

....

2. *Setze die Präposition* ***to/with*** *an die richtige Stelle.*

a) The girl with the long black hair ...., is .... the one .... who .... he .... danced ....

b) The party .... which .... we .... went .... was .... very .... good ....

c) Most of the girls .... that .... he .... danced .... were .... not .... as .... pretty.

11. Konjunktionen

1

Bindewörter: and, but, or, so, because

Um Hauptsätze und andere Satzteile miteinander zu verbinden, verwendest du im Englischen **and**, **but**, **or**, **so** und **because**. Hauptsätze, die durch solche Bindewörter verbunden sind, werden durch ein Komma getrennt, es sei denn, sie sind sehr kurz.

We had a lovely holiday in Spain, and we decided to go there again.
We went there and we loved it.

2

1. *Setze das passende Verbindungswort ein.*

a) I have four sisters and four brothers, ... we all live together in a very big house.

b) She doesn't want to eat the cake, ... she doesn't like strawberries.

c) We could watch a movie, ... we could go outside.

2. *Verbinde die beiden Sätze durch das passende Verbindungswort. Schreibe in dein Heft.*

a) Hannah has a cold. She won't go to the beach today.
b) Jessy knows many things. She doesn't know the answer to that question.
c) Ben's team is very good. They work very hard.

3. *Sage auf Englisch, dass …*

a) du heute nicht in die Schule gehst weil du krank bist.

....

b) Tom einen Film sehen kann oder sich mit Ben treffen kann.

....

4. *Lies den Text. Nun schreibe ihn um, indem du Bindewörter einsetzt, um ihn flüssiger zu machen. Schreibe in dein Heft.*

One evening I was alone at home. Mum told me to read a nice book. She told me to go to bed early. I watched a scary movie. Suddenly I heard a sound outside. I went to the window. It was dark. I could not see anything. I quickly hid behind the sofa. I was very scared. Then I heard my father's voice: "Benjam Thomas Miller! Where are you and why is the TV on?" I was happy to hear my father's voice.

Test

3

1. *Setze die passenden Verbindungswörter ein.*

a) I don't have any homework, ... I can meet my friends this afternoon.

b) We will go to the movies, ... then we can go and have dinner somewhere.

c) Would you like a sausage, ... do you prefer a steak?

2. *Sage auf Englisch, dass …*

a) deine Mutter heute spät nachhause kommt, weil sie länger arbeitet.

....

b) das Telefon klingelte und du daher drangegangen bist. (to answer the phone)

....

Konjunktionen

1

Konjunktionen: because, because of, when

Weitere wichtige Konjunktionen sind:

because	weil	I can't come **because** it's late.
because of	wegen	**Because of** you, I can't come back.
when	als wenn	**When** I saw that I laughed. **When** she hears that she will laugh.

2

1. *Sieh dir die Satzteile an, sortiere sie und bilde Sätze, indem du die passenden Konjunktionen verwendest.*

a) two days ago/Grandpa and I/climbed up a hill/the weather was great

....

....

b) reached the top of the hill/looked up at the sky/saw black clouds

....

....

c) strong rain/I could not see/I think there was/a lonely figure/standing on a rock

....

....

2. *Finde die Fehler und korrigiere den ganzen Satz.*

a) Wenn the rain stopped, the figure was gone.

....

b) Because of I wanted to know who the man was, I asked an old lady.

....

c) She said, that he was a ghost and because a lost love he always came out in the rain.

....

....

3. *Sage auf Englisch, dass …*

a) du wegen des Regens nicht richtig sehen konntest.

....

b) der Mann im Regen stand wegen einer verlorenen Liebe.

....

c) die Sonne schien, als es aufhörte zu regnen.

....

4. *Erfinde Sätze.*

a) Because of you ....

....

b) .... because

....

c) When ....

....

Konjunktionen

5. *Verbinde die beiden Sätze zu einem Satz mithilfe von Konjunktionen. Zum Teil musst du die Sätze auch ein wenig verändern, damit es passt.*

a) I love Christmas. My whole family will be home. ....

....

b) The weather was bad. We went home. ....

....

c) Anna will visit me tomorrow. We will go to the beach. ....

....

6. *Finde die Fehler und korrigiere den ganzen Satz.*

a) If he said, that I was wrong I became angry. ....

....

b) I never eat seafood because of I don't like the taste. ....

....

c) I was happy because the lovely surprise. ....

....

7. *Frage auf Englisch, ob …*

a) sie wegen dir zu spät kam.

Was she late ....

....?

b) er das Buch vergessen hat weil er in Eile war.

Did he forget the book ....

....?

Test

1. *Setze die Konjunktionen sinnvoll ein.*

a) .... he saw the man in the rain, Ben immediately told his grandfather.

b) .... Ben came home he told his sister the story.

c) .... Anne doesn't believe in ghosts, she did not believe Ben.

2. *Sage auf Englisch, dass …*

a) du wegen mir lachen musstest.

....

b) du nachhause musst, weil es spät ist.

....

c) du schlafen gegangen bist, als es dunkel wurde.

....

3. *Finde die Fehler und korrigiere den ganzen Satz.*

a) I did this because you.

....

b) She finds out when, she will be angry.

....

c) We didn't buy any nuts, because my allergy.

....

Konjunktionen

1

Konjunktionen Zeit, Bedingung, Gegensatz, Ursache

Konjunktionen machen logische Beziehungen deutlich. Sie können beispielsweise zeitliche Beziehungen deutlich machen (Was war vorher? später? gleichzeitig?).
Weitere wichtige Konjunktionen sind:

Zeit	**after, before, when, while, since, until**
Bedingung	**if, unless, only if, whether or not, even if**
Gegensatz	**although, though, even though, whereas, while**
Ursache	**because, since, now that, as, in order to**

2

1. *Fülle die Lücken mit einer passenden Konjunktion.*

a) We waited .... it was dark.

b) My brother wants to be firefighter .... he grows up.

c) Becka came to school, ... she was not feeling well.

2. *Verbinde die Sätze durch sinnvolle Konjunktionen.*

a) I went to see that movie. I am scared of wolves.

....

b) I won't go to the beach. I don't feel better.

....

c) You should think .... you speak.

....

3. *Sage auf Englisch, dass …*

a) es nach dem Sturm ruhig war.

....

b) du nach Amerika fliegen wirst, obwohl du Angst vorm Fliegen hast.

....

c) du nach Amerika fliegst, weil deine beste Freundin da wohnt.

....

4. *Richtig oder falsch? Kreuze an.*

	R	F
a) Since we are here anyway, we can enjoy it.	☐	☐
b) When you like, we can go to Edinburgh.	☐	☐
c) I want to go to the Festival because it is famous.	☐	☐

5. *Setze sinnvolle Konjunktionen ein.*

It was dark. .... they couldn't see anything, the five friends quietly moved forward. They would not leave the island .... they had found out about its secret. "................................ we are here, we need a plan!" said George. .... solve the mystery of the missing artifacts they had traveled far from home. "We should have thought of a plan .... we came to a lonely island in the middle of the night!" grumbled Dick. .... they liked it, they did not have a plan so far but there was somebody on this island who

Konjunktionen

had a plan. And it wasn't for them. "We'll think of something. Hey, I know! Alright, come over here and listen." Anne always had the best ideas.

6. *Frage auf Englisch, ob …*

a) ob ich nach dem Film eine Pizza essen will. ....

....?

b) du nur nach Amerika fliegen kannst, wenn du deinen Pass hast.

Can I travel to America ....

....?

c) du Wanderschuhe brauchst, um auf den Trip zu gehen.

Do I need hiking boots ....

....?

3 Test

1. *Verbinde die Sätze durch sinnvolle Konjunktionen.*

a) You come home early. Please make some tea.

....

....

b) We can hire the bike for two weeks. It is very cheap.

....

....

c) It is very cold. The sun is shining.

....

2. *Fülle die Lücken im Text, indem du entsprechende Konjunktionen einsetzt.*

Edinburgh has a long history .... it is a very old city. .... the Edinburgh Festival starts, thousands of people come to the city. .... not many people speak Gaelic, some of the plays at the Festival are in that old language.

.... the festival is now one of the most important festivals of music and drama, many people know about it.

.... the city is one of Europe's main cultural centres, there are many artists who live here.

3. *Beantworte die Fragen mithilfe der Konjunktionen.*

a) How long have you been waiting for?

I have been waiting .... this morning.

b) Why do you want to go to the Edinburgh Festival?

.... I read a fascinating story about it.

c) What is your opinion on ghosts?

I think I saw one, ... I don't believe in ghosts.

Kapitel 1: Verben

Seite 6

1. a) (to) listen; listened; listened b) (to) work; worked; worked
   c) (to) look; looked; looked d) (to) stop; stopped; stopped
   e) (to) want; wanted; wanted f) (to) use; used; used

Seite 7

2. a) used; b) carried; c) kissed; d) wanted; e) liked

3. a) (to) use; b) (to) carry; c) (to) kiss; d) (to) want; e) (to) like

4. a) My brother played tennis yesterday.
   b) My sister listened to music.
   c) My father cooked lunch.
   d) My mother watched TV.
   e) My dog wanted to eat.
   f) I loved my family.

Seite 8

5. go come want play see take live run
   laugh sing drink eat buy sell cry
   shout become be love

6. want; wanted; wanted
   play; played; played
   live; lived; lived
   laugh; laughed; laughed
   cry; cried; cried
   shout; shouted; shouted
   love; loved; loved

7. a) I play tennis. b) I laugh when I see funny films.
   c) I want an ice cream, please.
   d) I love my family. e) I live in London.
   f) I always cry when my grandmother goes away.
   g) I don't want to shout at my brother.

Seite 9

Test

1.

S	S	E	D	I	S	C	O	F	O	L
S	E	E	N	S	A	W	B	C	M	O
L	L	I	S	T	E	N	E	D	G	O
I	O	P	L	A	Y	E	D	K	A	K
V	R	E	C	L	U	E	V	I	D	A
E	W	O	R	K	X	D	I	S	N	X
B	O	L	A	E	B	Y	D	S	E	F
U	S	O	T	D	H	Q	E	Q	V	I
D	T	H	E	O	S	P	O	B	T	H

a) play; b) talk; c) need; d) kiss
e) look; f) work; g) listen; h) live

2.	a) (to) work	worked	worked
	b) (to) love	loved	loved
	c) (to) carry	carried	carried
	d) (to) want	wanted	wanted
	e) (to) look	looked	looked
	f) (to) phone	phoned	phoned

Auswertung zum Test
Bei Aufgabe 1 bekommst du für jedes gefundene Wort einen Punkt.
Bei Aufgabe 2 bringt jede richtig gefüllte Lücke einen Punkt.

Von insgesamt 20 Punkten hast du .... Punkte erreicht.

Super!	In Ordnung!	Bitte noch einmal üben!
20 bis 17 Punkte	16 bis 12 Punkte	Weniger als 12 Punkte

Seite 11

1.	(to) be	was/were	be (been)
	(to) buy	buyed (bought)	bought
	(to) came (come)	come (came)	come
	(to) drink	drink (drank)	drinked (drunk)

2.	a) become	became	become
	b) buy	brought	bought
	c) drink	drank	drunk
	d) feel	felt	felt
	e) hear	heard	heard
	f) lose	lost	lost

3.	feel ▲	work ■	listen ■
	make ▲	become ▲	look ■

Seite 12

4. Zu korrigieren waren:
   1 were 2 invented 3 wrote 4 were
   5 made 6 directed 7 acted 8 are

5.	feel	felt	felt
	see	saw	seen
	make	made	made

Seite 13

Test

1.	a) forget	forgot	forgotten
	b) give	gave	given
	c) drink	drank	drunk
	d) know	knew	known
	e) begin	began	begun
	f) fly	flew	flown

2. Dear Liza
We are now in Spain. Finally my summer holidays can begin. We arrived late at night and it was dark. We looked for our hotel but all the names were in Spanish, so we stopped and asked an old man for directions. He spoke to us in Spanish, so we had to guess what he meant. Then my father saw a big sign with the name of our hotel. This morning I woke up to the sound of the waves and the seagulls. Holidays – here I come!
Yours Melinda

Auswertung zum Test
Bei Aufgabe 1 bekommst du für jedes gefundene Wort einen Punkt.
Bei Aufgabe 2 bringt jede richtig gefüllte Lücke einen Punkt.

Von insgesamt 23 Punkten hast du .... Punkte erreicht.

Super!	In Ordnung!	Bitte noch einmal üben!
23 bis 20 Punkte	19 bis 13 Punkte	Weniger als 13 Punkte

Seite 15

1. a) There is a new girl in our class.
   b) There are some crayons in the cupboard.
   c) There is a lot of noise!
   d) There is a spider in my bag.

2. a) There was a new girl in our class.
   b) There were some crayons in the cupboard.
   c) There was a lot of noise!
   d) There was a spider in my bag.

Seite 16

3. Mum: What is wrong Lena?
Lena: I can't find my ipod. Where is it?
Mum: Does your brother have your ipod in his bed?
Lena: No, he hasn't. Very strange, Mum.
Mum: I really don't know. Do Laura and Ella have an ipod, too?
Lena: No, they don't. They have an old CD-player.
Hm. Maybe they have my ipod?
Mum: Let's look in their room. – Yes, they have got it!

4. a) Do you often get together with your friends on the weekends?
   b) Ivy does her homework every day.
   c) Did the teacher forget her book again yesterday?
   d) Does your mother go to work every day?
   e) He always does the dishes.
   f) How many paper planes do you build every day?

Seite 17

5. a) What do you want to do tomorrow?
   b) Why does she always scream like that?
   c) Where have you been?
   d) How much did these earrings cost?
   e) What has he got in that bag?
   f) Why do I look like this?

g) When did they arrive home?

6. a) I have got a pony.
   b) Do you have a pony, too?
   c) What have you done?
   d) How does he know about it?
   e) Do you like ice-cream?
   f) Who has got the tickets?

7. Dear Diary,
   There is something I must tell you! I do not have a lot of time, but I will try to tell you quickly. Last week there was a flea market in town. Remember, that I saw this beautiful red bike at my friend's house some time ago? Well, there were many people at the market and they had many different things to sell. Suddenly Daddy said: "Do you see that red bike?" Of course I saw it! And guess what?
   I have got a red bike now. My friend has got a green bike. Sometimes there are some really nice things at flea markets!

Test Seite 18

1. a) Do you like animals?
   b) Does she have a pony?
   c) When do you do your homework?
   d) Why did she scream?
   e) Who has the tickets?
   f) Where did you go?

2. a) There is a flea market in town! Seite 19
   b) There are many things to see at a flea market.
   c) There are no bikes under that Christmas tree!
   d) There were a lot of bikes at her friend's house.
   e) There was a lovely red bike at the flea market.
   f) There is always a surprise waiting for you!

3. a) I do my homework every day.
   b) My friend has got a new dog.
   c) There were many people at the flea market.

4. a) Does she live in London?
   b) What does she know?
   c) Why does he always scream (like that)?

5.

When did	you been?
There is	we do about this?
Who has got	many people at a flea market?
What do	a lot of homework today.
Where have	you find out?
Are there	an idea?

Verben

Auswertung zum Test
Ziehe dir für jeden Fehler einen Punkt ab.

Von insgesamt 23 Punkten hast du .... Punkte erreicht.

Super!	In Ordnung!	Bitte noch einmal üben!
23 bis 20 Punkte	19 bis 14 Punkte	Weniger als 14 Punkte

Seite 21

1. a) simple present b) present progressive
   c) simple present d) present progressive
   e) simple present f) present progressive

2. Hello, my name is Anne. I speak German and English. My parents are from Germany, but we live in London. My brother, Tim, is six years old and he loves London. He thinks it is very exciting. His favorite place is London Zoo. I like London but I miss my old home in Germany. We often go to visit our grandmother Elisabeth.

Seite 22

3. a) Ben likes carrots, but he doesn't like tomatoes.
   b) I play tennis, but I don't play golf.
   c) We live in England, we don't live in Germany.
   d) Tim has got a dog, he doesn't have a cat.

4. a) I live in Germany.
   b) My friend doesn't like bananas.
   c) My younger brother is six years old.

Seite 23

5. a) Does your father's friend speak English and German?
   b) Do your friends want pizza?
   c) Does Chantal speak French?

6. a) At the moment I am standing in the rain.
   b) Benjamin plays basketball every Thursday.
   c) Mum and Dad are playing tennis now.
   d) I never eat salad!
   e) Do you like chocolate?

Seite 24

7. a) I am not sleeping.
   b) My family doesn't like football.
   c) You do not/don't go to London Zoo every day.
   d) My mother is not/isn't talking to a friend.
   e) Kate and Samira do not/don't collect everything about horses.
   f) The dog is not/isn't looking at you.

8. a) Is the gorilla drinking a cup of tea? No, it isn't. The gorilla is reading (a book).
   b) Is the bird reading? No, it isn't. The bird is singing.
   c) Is the dog kissing the cat? No, it isn't. The dog is playing with the cat.

Seite 25

Test

1. a) I help my mother every day.
   b) My sister is eating lunch at the moment.

2. a) Is my mother sleeping?
   b) Does Sarah watch TV every day?

3. a) Is Mum talking to her friend?
   b) Does the bear love salad?

4. a) Luka eats apples, but he doesn't/does not eat bananas.
   b) Anna is reading a book, she isn't/is not writing a book.

Auswertung zum Test
Hast du alles richtig? Dann bekommst du bei den Aufgaben 1 und 3 zwei Punkte je richtig gelöster Teilaufgabe. Bei Aufgabe 4 bekommst du einen Punkt pro Teilaufgabe.

Von insgesamt 14 Punkten hast du .... Punkte erreicht.

Super!	In Ordnung!	Bitte noch einmal üben!
14 bis 13 Punkte	12 bis 9 Punkte	Weniger als 9 Punkte

Seite 26

1. a) Yesterday I went to see my best friend.
   b) There we met some friends and a dog.
   c) We all played football.
   d) We had to stop because the dog ate the ball.

2. a) Benjamin had a dog.
   b) We lived in London.
   c) My parents didn't go to New York.
   d) I wrote a letter to my grandmother.

Seite 27

3. a) I was at school yesterday.
   b) Layla didn't go to school last week.
   c) The teacher was ill.

4. a) Was Timmy at school yesterday?
   b) Did I do my homework yesterday?
   c) Did Mike like lunch?

Seite 28

5. 300 years ago I lived in a big castle in Ireland. My parents were wise and had a good heart. I did not have brothers or sisters. I played on my own most of the time. But one day something terrible happened.
   There was a big fire and I was the only one who died. Because I miss my family so much, I still live in the castle today.

6. Anna and her family went to Scotland every year. At the moment they are visiting a friend, Mr McVarady who lives in an old castle. At the moment Anne is talking to Mr McVaraday. Anna: "Mr McVarady, do you live here alone?"
   "Yes, Anne", says Mr McVarady. "I live here alone. Well, not really, because there is Bernadette. She is the White Lady. She is a ghost. She lived here 300 years ago and had a sad life. But you don't have to be afraid. She is a friendly ghost."
   Anna doesn't like ghosts. Yesterday she saw a lady in the garden! She ran away at once!

Verben

Seite 29

7. a + 5; b + 4; c + 2; d + 1; e + 3; f + 6

8. a) Did you watch a movie yesterday?
   b) When did Ben come home yesterday?
   c) Were you at home yesterday?
   d) Did you meet Sally at the cinema?

9.

		R	F
a)	He carryd her home.	☐	☑
b)	Yesterday we went to the cinema.	☑	☐
c)	Chip lives many years ago.	☐	☑

Seite 30

Test

1 a) Chip lived 300 years ago.
  b) Chips parents were nice people.
  c) Chip didn't like dogs.
  d) Anna saw a woman in the garden.
  e) Mr McVarady met the White Lady.
  f) Anna talked to the White Lady.

2. a) Anna ate ice cream (with her parents).
   b) Anna went to a castle./Anna saw a castle./Anna visited a castle.
   c) Anna saw the White Lady./Anna met the White Lady (in the garden).
   d) Anna swam (in the sea).

Seite 31

3. My family lives in London. Our house is very old. My grandmother always says that there is a ghost in the bedroom upstairs. She can often hear the ghost at night. Last year, the ghost spoke to her. My grandmother tells me that story sometimes. At the moment I am sitting in the old bedroom and I am waiting for the ghost to come and speak to me.

Auswertung zum Test

Für jede richtig gelöste Teilaufgabe und für jede richtig gefüllte Lücke bekommst du einen Punkt.

Von insgesamt 18 Punkten hast du .... Punkte erreicht.

Super!	In Ordnung!	Bitte noch einmal üben!
18 bis 16 Punkte	15 bis 11 Punkte	Weniger als 11 Punkte

Seite 33

1. a) I have played/Have I played?
   b) She has gone/Has she gone?
   c) You have been/Have you been?
   d) He has become/Has he become?
   e) We have visited/Have we visited?

2. a) I have never been to America.
   b) I have just washed my hands.
   c) She has seen Ben.

3 a) Has he ever been to Africa?
   b) Has Tina lived in Brighton for five years?
   c) Has Jimmy played Rugby since 2013?

Seite 34

4. a) The cat has slept for two hours.
   b) I haven't done my homework yet.
   c) Has she ever/never been to England?

5. Carla has got a friend in America. She has wanted to visit her for three years now. Last week Carla arrived in New York. On her first day Carla was very excited about all the interesting things you can see and do in New York! She hasn't been to the Empire State Building, yet, but she has already seen some important sights of New York.
   A few days ago her host-family took her to visit a famous museum, the Museum of Modern Art and Carla loved the paintings she saw there.
   Yesterday morning her mother called her from Germany.
   "Tell me about the things you have done since last week!" she said. Carla told her everything.
   "We have just booked some tickets for Disney World!" she said, "I am so excited!"

Seite 35

Test

1. She has visited the Modern Art Museum.
   She hasn't taken pictures of the Empire State Building.
   She has spent some time at the New York Zoo.
   She has visited the Statue of Liberty.
   She hasn't gone to Disney World.

2 a) Have you had a cup of tea?
   b) Have you lived in New York for five years?
   c) Have they bought a new car?

Auswertung zum Test

Hast du alles richtig? Dann hast du 8 Punkte. Ziehe dir für jeden Fehler einen Punkt ab.

Von insgesamt 8 Punkten hast du .... Punkte erreicht.

Super!	In Ordnung!	Bitte noch einmal üben!
8 Punkte	7 bis 6 Punkte	Weniger als 6 Punkte

Seite 36

1. a) Benjamin was eating a bar of chocolate.
   b) Tina and Megan were looking at a magazine.
   c) Andy was copying math homework from Ben.
   d) Class 6 was playing basketball in the gym.
   e) Anna was chatting with her neighbour.

Seite 37

2. ☑ The weather was changing quickly. –
☐ I stood at my window. – ☑ The storm was coming closer. –
☑ My father and my mother were searching for candles. –
☐ Jenny wasn't in her room. – ☑ Was she hiding somewhere? –
☐ Did she go outside? – ☑ When the first thunder crashed, I was calling her name.
☑ It was getting darker and darker. –
☐ I heard footsteps behind me. – ☐ Was it Jenny? –
☑ Yes, and she was smiling at me!

3. a) Mrs Nosy, were you watching TV when you heard the alarm?
b) Mr Roundabout, was your wife washing her hair when you saw the young man?
c) What were you doing in the living room, Mr Careless?
d) Was the maid cleaning the windows when you heard the scream, Lady Goosebumps?
e) Butler James, where were Mr and Mrs White when you were speaking to the stranger?
f) Mr and Mrs White, were you playing the piano together when Butler James came in?

Seite 38

4. a) Will wasn't sleeping in his bed. He was standing at the window.
b) The wind was howling. It wasn't blowing softly.
c) The dog was hiding under the bed. It wasn't sleeping in front of the fireplace.
d) The cat wasn't hunting mice. It was sitting on Will's bed.

5. a) Who were Grandma and Grandpa helping?
b) Who was cooking noodles?
c) Where was Anna sleeping?
d) What were the children playing?

Seite 39

6. a) Mr Cooper was talking to some girls from class 5.
b) James, John and Jordan were playing basketball.
c) Bridget was writing a math test.
d) Class 8 was watching a DVD about the life of whales.
e) Mrs Nelson was looking for Simon.

7. a) I was tidying my room while my mother did the shopping/was shopping.
b) My parents were watching a movie when I heard the noise/the sound.

8. a) Was Ben in the living room when the lights went out?
b) Was Sherlock Holmes smoking his pipe when Watson met him?
c) Was the cat drinking milk when the dog came into the house?

Seite 40

9. a) She was playing in the garden while he cooked lunch.
b) Mrs Donovan was watching TV when the storm began.
c) Mr Donovan was reading a book when the storm began.

10.

	R	F
a) They was in the classroom, when the fire alarm went off.	☐	☑
b) She read a book, when he came home.	☐	☑

Test Seite 41

1. a) You: "No, she wasn't doing her homework. Anna was doing her homework."
   b) You: "No, they weren't. Hannes and Christian were eating sandwiches."
   c) You: "No, he wasn't. Helena was talking to her friends."

2. Pascal: "I was daydreaming about my favourite rock star."
   Louisa: "I was looking at my fingernails."
   Tom: "I was trying to solve a personal problem."
   Raffael: "I was standing in front of the fire alarm button."

Auswertung zum Test
Hast du alles richtig? Dann hast du 7 Punkte. Ziehe dir für jeden Fehler einen Punkt ab.

Von insgesamt 7 Punkten hast du .... Punkte erreicht.

Super!	In Ordnung!	Bitte noch einmal üben!
7 Punkte	6 bis 5 Punkte	Weniger als 5 Punkte

Seite 42

1. a) Ah, Anna, you will travel around the world.
   b) At first, you will not have/won't have a lot of money, but then things will change for the better.
   c) You will find the perfect job.
   d) In Paris you will meet a handsome, young man.
   e) He will fall in love with you.

Seite 43

2. a) I think I am going to buy more chocolate ice-cream.
   b) Oh, I have eaten too much. I am afraid I will be sick!
   c) I am not going to go on the roller coaster.
   d) Tonight I am going to drink chamomile tea.
   e) Oh, look at that man spitting fire! He will burn himself!
   f) Oh, they also sell candy floss. I am feeling better already, so I am going to have some.

3. a) I think it will rain.
   b) I am going to go to a birthday party.

Seite 44

4. a) Is Anna going to go on the ghost train?
   b) Won't Pascal be afraid?
   c) Is Anna going to eat another Hamburger?
   d) Are my parents going to pick me up?

5. a) The roller coaster looks scary so I am not going to go up.
   b) The candy floss is delicious but Anna is not going to have more.

6. a) I feel terrible. I think I ~~am going to~~/**will** be sick.
   b) Look at those clouds! It ~~is going to~~/**will** rain any minute.
   c) We have a free evening so we **are going to**/~~will~~ see Shrek.
   d) Do you think Luka **is going to**/~~will~~ visit us today?
   e) I am easily scared, so I **am not going to**/~~won't~~ go on the ghost train.

7. a) John won't hurt himself.
   b) Eliza is not going to meet her friend tomorrow.

Seite 45 Test

1. a) The ghost train will be scary.
   b) She won't go on the roller coaster.
   c) We are going to see the new movie.
   d) It will rain.

2. Beispiellösung
   a) Anna is going to fly to Los Angeles.
   b) Anna is going to meet the James Bond actor.
   c) Anna is going to show him her skateboard stunts.
   d) Anna is going to get a part in the film.

3. a) He will not/won't find the keys.
   b) It will not/won't snow soon.
   c) They are not going to buy me a present.

Auswertung zum Test

Für jede richtig gelöste Teilaufgabe bekommst du einen Punkt. Bei Aufgabe 2 kannst du auch anders formuliert haben. Achte dann darauf, dass du „is going to“ verwendet hast.

Von insgesamt 11 Punkten hast du .... Punkte erreicht.

Super!	In Ordnung!	Bitte noch einmal üben!
11 bis 10 Punkt	9 bis 7 Punkte	Weniger als 7 Punkte

Seite 46

1. a) My bike had disappeared.
   b) Our coach had helped us.
   c) The championship had been lost.
   d) Her tennis racket had broken.
   e) The horse had won the race.
   f) The Stuntman had lost his nerve.

Seite 47

2. senkrecht / waagrecht

senkrecht	waagrecht
1 come	1 been
2 found	2 dug
3 caught	3 cut
4 drawn	4 forgotten

3. b) Our coach had not helped us before we went into camp.
   c) The championship had not been lost when they scored the first goal.
   d) Her tennis racket had not broken before she finished the match.

Seite 48

4. a) My training had not ended when I went home.
   b) Before the foul play happened the team had lost.
   c) After I caught the ball I threw it to Ben.
   d) I had known the new rules before I entered the game.
   e) After I had left the swimming pool it started to rain.
   f) Sam had warned me before I hurt myself.

Test

1. a) eaten b) bitten
   c) drawn d) thought
   e) caught f) forgotten
   g) chosen h) become

2. a) Tom had gone out when his girlfriend called. Seite 49
   b) Had he left a message for her?
   c) No, he had written a note before he left.
   d) Had she been angry about that?
   e) Yes, she had been angry at first.
   f) But when she saw, what he had bought her, she smiled.

3. a) After we had seen the finals of the football championship in Brazil, we flew back home.
   b) My mother had booked our flights before we left for the finals.
   c) We had arrived at the airport, when Mum started looking for the tickets.
   d) She had put everything in her handbag, but now she could not find them.
   d) My father had watched her for a while, before he said: "I have the tickets in my jacket, because I did not want you to lose them."

Auswertung zum Test

Für jede richtig gelöste Teilaufgabe bekommst du einen Punkt.

Von insgesamt 19 Punkten hast du .... Punkte erreicht.

Super!	In Ordnung!	Bitte noch einmal üben!
19 bis 17 Punkt	16 bis 11 Punkte	Weniger als 11 Punkte

1. I must stay at home today because I am sick. The doctor said I can't go to school. He said that I needn't stay in bed the whole time. But I mustn't do too much, because my head hurts. So I need to wait until I feel better before I can go out to meet my friends. Seite 50

2. a) I needn't do homework today. b) We can play football.
   c) He must win this match. d) Tim mustn't go outside.
   e) I can't do this.

3. a) You must stay in bed, because you are very sick! Seite 51
   b) She can't stay in bed, because she has to go to school.
   c) I needn't stay in bed, because the doctor said I should go for walks.
   d) We can stay in bed, because it's Sunday.
   e) They mustn't stay in bed, because it's Monday morning!

4. a) I can play the piano.
   b) We needn't do any homework today.
   c) I can't sing well.

5. a) Christian and Joe can watch TV in the afternoon but they mustn't watch TV at night. Seite 52
   b) They can eat food from the fridge but the mustn't buy sweets.

c) They can go to Ben's birthday party but they mustn't come home after 7 o'clock.
d) They can ride their bikes but they mustn't go into town.

6. a) Children in Great Britain must wear school uniforms.
   b) Most children in Germany needn't wear school uniforms.
   c) Many children in Africa can't go to school, because they are poor.
   d) In some countries girls mustn't go to school.

Seite 53 Test

1. a) Tony can't write the test, because he has a headache.
   b) I must wait 30 minutes.
   c) She mustn't see the new movie/film.

2. Mum: "You needn't help me with the dishes, we have a dishwasher! But go and do your homework!"
   Andy: "Must I do my homework now? I want to meet Jill in five minutes!"
   Mum:" No, please finish them first. Oh dear! The children mustn't play football on the lawn over there! Mr. Grumble will shout at them.
   Andy:" I can go and tell them and save them!"
   Mum:" No, you can't. You must do your homework now. I will tell them myself."

Auswertung zum Test
Bei Aufgabe 1 bekommst du für jede richtige Übersetzung einen Punkt.
Bei Aufgabe 2 bringt jede richtig gefüllte Lücke einen Punkt.

Von insgesamt 9 Punkten hast du .... Punkte erreicht.

Super!	In Ordnung!	Bitte noch einmal üben!
9 bis 8 Punkte	7 bis 5 Punkte	Weniger als 5 Punkte

Seite 54 1.

Sie darf nicht rennen.	I needn't buy bread.
Er kann Fahrrad fahren.	We have to see this!
Ich muss kein Brot kaufen.	She is not allowed to run.
Wir müssen das sehen!	I can't think.
Ich kann nicht nachdenken.	He is able to ride a bike.

2. a) You didn't have to help me.
   b) Were the children allowed to watch a DVD?
   c) You mustn't shout.

Seite 55

3. a) Can we have a coke? Yes, but you must drink it before we get on the bus. People mustn't drink anything in the bus.
   b) Yesterday my little sister had to pay the full prize. Only children which are ten years and above needn't pay the full prize.

4. a) Benjamin wasn't allowed to buy chocolate.
   b) We had to find a way out.
   c) She didn't have to say anything.

5. a) Yesterday I had to tell my parents the truth.
   b) They are allowed to go to the party.
   c) She didn't have to run away.

Seite 56

6. Many years ago, a young man took his boat out on a lake. He wasn't able to swim, but he was brave (mutig). The people in his village said: "You mustn't take your boat on that lake! The lake monster is going to come and get you!" He knew that he didn't have to go, but he wanted to find a treasure. He couldn't swim, but he was able to hold his breath for a very long time. "I have to find the treasure. Only then Lady Gwen will marry me!" he said to his dog. He put a rope around his dog and himself and told his dog, that he had to run and pull when the signal came. So the young man jumped into the lake and his dog had to pull him out.

Seite 57

Test

1. a) Oh no! Did I have to buy milk?
   No, you didn't have to buy milk.
   b) Were you able to do your homework with a headache?
   No, I wasn't able to.
   c) Was Anna allowed to go swimming?
   No, she wasn't.

2.

a)	Are we allowed to sit here?	Verbot
b)	Visitors mustn't feed the animals.	Erlaubnis
c)	Ben was able to run faster than Tom.	Fähigkeit

3. a) I was allowed to talk to her when she came home.
   b) Did they have to brush their teeth before dinner?
   c) I had to buy bread.

Auswertung zum Test

Bei Aufgabe 1 bekommst du für jede richtig übersetzte Frage und für jede richtig gebildete Verneinung einen Punkt. Hier sind also sechs Punkte möglich. Bei Aufgabe 2 bekommst für jede richtige Verbindung ebenfalls einen Punkt. Bei Aufgabe 3 bringt jede richtig gelöste Teilaufgabe einen Punkt.

Von insgesamt 12 Punkten hast du .... Punkte erreicht.

Super!	In Ordnung!	Bitte noch einmal üben!
12 bis 10 Punkte	9 bis 7 Punkte	Weniger als 7 Punkte

Seite 58

1. a) You were supposed to do your homework now.
   b) Was she allowed to go outside with the children?
   c) You were supposed to read this book for your project.

2. a) We ought to save water.
   b) Alice may see the Queen.
   c) Anna should open the window, to let in some fresh air.

Verben

Seite 59

Test

1. a) We should leave soon. ☑
   b) You were supposed to go. ☑
   c) Liz ought to call her mother. ☑

2. a) We were supposed to take off our shoes in here.
   b) Were we supposed to tell father about the test?
   c) You were supposed to apologize!

3. a) Emma may sit down.
   b) Jessica ought to listen.
   c) We shouldn't do that.

Auswertung zum Test

Ziehe dir für jeden Fehler einen Punkt ab.

Von insgesamt 9 Punkten hast du …….. Punkte erreicht.

Super!	In Ordnung!	Bitte noch einmal üben!
9 bis 8 Punkte	7 bis 5 Punkte	Weniger als 5 Punkte

Seite 60

1. a Swimming is not allowed here. / No swimming
   b) Smoking is not allowed here. / No smoking
   c) Fishing is not allowed here. / No fishing

2. a) Anna loves dancing.
   b) I don't like hiking.

Seite 61

3. a) Staying in bed on a Sunday morning is wonderful.
   b) Anna loves baking. Her cakes are very good.
   c) I like doing sports but I think cycling is horrible.

4. a) Playing basketball is my hobby.
   b) I like reading.
   c) I think fishing is boring.

Test

1. a) Swimming is fun.
   b) Benjamin and Finn like playing computer games.

2. a) Peter and Tom can't stand dancing.
   b) They think dancing is stupid.
   c) But Sophie loves dancing.
   d) Playing football is her other hobby.

Auswertung zum Test
Ziehe dir für jeden Fehler einen Punkt ab.

Von insgesamt 6 Punkten hast du .... Punkte erreicht.

Super!	In Ordnung!	Bitte noch einmal üben!
6 Punkte	5 bis 4 Punkte	Weniger als 4 Punkte

Seite 62

1. a) He/The boy is good at baking cakes.
   b) She/The girl is good at taking photographs.
   c) He/The boy is good at speaking Spanish.

Seite 63

2. a) I was afraid of losing my way.
   b) She was sorry about breaking that window.
   c) We were tired of talking about the problem.
   d) Are you interested in buying this smartphone?

3. Tim is good at climbing. He is interested in looking at snakes and other reptiles. He is not interested in horse riding. He can't stand seeing mice.

Test

1. a) I'm excited about going to Paris.
   b) I'm afraid of seeing snakes.
   c) She is tired of listening to you.
   d) He is happy about meeting Anna.

2. a) My father is used to working in the garden.
   b) Luka is good at making people smile.
   c) We are interested in sailing.

Auswertung zum Test
Ziehe dir für jeden Fehler einen Punkt ab.

Von insgesamt 7 Punkten hast du .... Punkte erreicht.

Super!	In Ordnung!	Bitte noch einmal üben!
7 bis 6 Punkte	5 bis 4 Punkte	Weniger als 4 Punkte

Kapitel 2: Präpositionen

Seite 64

1. a) I was born in 2003.
   b) Can we meet on Monday?

Seite 65

2. a) Sabrina's birthday is March, 24th./ Sabrina was born on the 24th. of March.
   b) My father was born in 1975.

3.
Monday, Tuesday, Wednesday, Thursday, Friday, Saturday, Sunday

January, February, March, April
May, June, July, August
September, October, November, December

Test

1. a) I'll visit my aunt at the weekend (BE)/on the weekend (AE).
   b) Ben doesn't have time at the moment.
   c) I drink tea in the morning.

2. a) I can't sleep at night.
   b) Today is September, 5th.
   c) We are in France in August.

Auswertung zum Test

Ziehe dir für jeden Fehler einen Punkt ab.

Von insgesamt 6 Punkten hast du …….. Punkte erreicht.

Super!	In Ordnung!	Bitte noch einmal üben!
6 Punkte	5 bis 4 Punkte	Weniger als 4 Punkte

Seite 67

1. a) 500 years ago people did not have cars.
   b) She has played the cello for 5 years.

2. a) Can you put that picture on the wall?
   b) My uncle from Australia is coming. We are waiting at the airport.
   c) I found this picture in a magazine.

Test

1. Dear Grandma, we have been in London since last Monday and I have seen a lot! Did you know that Richard Lionheart lived almost a 1000 years ago? We were at a theater to see a special show about him and the people of his time. Posters about this show were on every bus and train. During the show Dad had to go to the restrooms, because he forgot to go before the show. Mum was angry with him! And did you know that London is on the Thames? That river is quite smelly! Yours Anna

Auswertung zum Test

Gib dir für jede richtig eingesetzte Präposition einen Punkt.

Von insgesamt 7 Punkten hast du .... Punkte erreicht.

Super!	In Ordnung!	Bitte noch einmal üben!
7 bis 6 Punkte	5 bis 4 Punkte	Weniger als 4 Punkte

Seite 68

1. a) My father walked through the desert.
   b) Lucy is from England.

2. a) If you want to get there, you must climb over the wall.
   b) The hospital is next to the parking lot.
   c) I said to him: "Be quiet!"

Seite 69

3. a) to travel around the world
   b) pick up fast food at a drive-through/ drive-in
   c) letters from/to Julia.

Test

1. Dear diary, yesterday I got a funny, old box from my mum. She told me that it was very, very old. Kings and queens had carried it through the country. There was a strange stone inside and over the stone lay a blue cloth. I took out the cloth and the stone and put the stone onto the cloth – but it didn't stay there. It always flew off the cloth and finally landed next to my foot. When I went to bed, I took the stone with me. But this morning the stone cracked open and suddenly there was a funny little animal beside me. I named it Arthur and he is my secret. I won't give him to anyone else!

2. a) The little animal was beside me.
   b) Somebody put a cloth over the stone.
   c) I went to bed and the stone cracked.

Auswertung zum Test

Ziehe dir für jeden Fehler einen Punkt ab.

Von insgesamt 11 Punkten hast du .... Punkte erreicht.

Super!	In Ordnung!	Bitte noch einmal üben!
11 bis 10 Punkte	9 bis 7 Punkte	Weniger als 7 Punkte

Kapitel 3: Nomen

Seite 70

1. a) What do I want?
   b) Do you speak German?
   c) Jo loves cats. But she hates spiders.

2. a) I live in England.
   b) Tom and Susie are my friends./are friends of mine.

Seite 71

3. horse book i queen tarzan
   you england german boy

4. Beispiellösung:
   I like ice cream. Jane likes Tarzan.
   I don't live in England. I speak German.

Test
1. This is Mr Jones. He lives in London. He has a daughter, Emma, and a son, Tom. They all like to go to the North of Scotland because they have a castle there.

Auswertung zum Test
Für jede richtige erkannte Korrekur gibt es einen Punkt.

Von insgesamt 7 Punkten hast du .... Punkte erreicht.

Super!	In Ordnung!	Bitte noch einmal üben!
7 bis 6 Punkte	5 bis 4 Punkte	Weniger als 4 Punkte

Seite 72

1.

S	P	A	R	T	S	F
T	E	E	T	H	K	D
D	O	N	U	I	L	F
H	P	Q	T	M	M	I
J	L	A	D	I	E	S
L	E	W	R	C	N	H
O	M	Y	F	E	V	E

a) parts
b) people
c) teeth
d) ladies
e) fish
f) mice
g) men

Seite 73

2. a) a pair of jeans b) tomatoes c) (two) cars
   d) (three) women e) (two) sheep

3. a) This is my new friend Rajan.
   b) These are my new shoes.
   c) These exercises are not easy!
   d) This boy is friendly.

Seite 74

4. a) This is Kathy's new dress and that are Kathy's old jeans.
   b) This is Kathy's new bag and that are her old backpacks.
   c) These are her new shoes and those are her old shoes.
   d) This is her new hat and those are her old hats.

5.

	R	F
a) These man is a thief!	☐	☑
b) This are not my books.	☐	☑
c) These are my new jeans.	☑	☐

Seite 75

Test

1. a) man b) police c) family

2. a) women b) windows c) hobbies
   d) shoes c) hours

3. a) Two children are playing in the garden.
   b) My friend has got many fish.
   c) White mice are prettier than grey mice.

Auswertung zum Test
Jede richtig gelöste Teilaufgabe ist einen Punkt wert.

Von insgesamt 11 Punkten hast du .... Punkte erreicht.

Super!	In Ordnung!	Bitte noch einmal üben!
11 bis 10 Punkte	9 bis 7 Punkte	Weniger als 7 Punkte

Seite 76

1. a) The red ones?
   b) The new one or the old one?

2. a) If you want comfortable shoes, take those ones.
   b) Look at that old car! – Which one? - That one.
   c) Ben loves marshmellows. He likes the white ones best.

3. a) the red apples one ☐ ones ☑
   b) the green bird one ☑ ones ☐
   c) the round glasses one ☐ ones ☑

4. a) I like my new hairstyle! I liked the old one better.
   b) She bought the wrong apples because I can't eat the green ones.

Seite 77

Test

1. Linda: "Mum, I saw really great shoes yesterday!"
   Ben: "Oh no, mum! She is talking about the ugly ones.
   Linda: "They were great! That T-shirt you bought was ugly."
   Ben: "Are you talking about the black one? "
   Linda: "Yes, that one. The ones we saw at the other shop were much nicer."

Nomen

2 a) The apples over there look really good. – The green ones?
b) I like my new teachers, but Mrs Jones is the best. – Is she the good-looking one?
c) Please give me that photo. – The black and white one?

3. a) the two blue fish — one ☐ ones ☑
b) one black sheep — one ☑ ones ☐
c) the red shoes — one ☐ ones ☑

Auswertung zum Test
Bei Aufgabe 1 gibt es für jede richtig gefüllte Lücke einen Punkt. Bei den Aufgaben 2 und 3 bekommst du für jede richtig gelöste Teilaufgabe einen Punkt.

Von insgesamt 10 Punkten hast du .... Punkte erreicht.

Super!	In Ordnung!	Bitte noch einmal üben!
10 bis 9 Punkte	8 bis 6 Punkte	Weniger als 6 Punkte

Seite 78

1. a) Rahel's pony b) Joshua's smartphone
c) Tom's comics

Seite 79

2. a) No, it's Joshua's.
b) No, they are Tom's.
c) Is this Tom's pony? No, it's Rahel's.

3.

	R	F
a) These are Linda's rabbits.	☑	☐
b) I love those shoe's.	☐	☑
c) Look at this test! Is it Ben's?	☑	☐

Test
1. Nelly and Louisa are shopping. They are looking at the shop windows.
Nelly's mobile phone rings. Her mother wants to know where she is.
Louisa's mother knows that the girls are in town. Nelly's sister forgot to tell their mother.

2. a) This is Tom's jacket.
b) There are many cars in my street.
c) Sam's mother is nice.

Auswertung zum Test
Ziehe dir für jeden Fehler einen Punkt ab.

Von insgesamt 8 Punkten hast du .... Punkte erreicht.

Super!	In Ordnung!	Bitte noch einmal üben!
8 bis 7 Punkte	6 bis 5 Punkte	Weniger als 5 Punkte

Seite 80

1. a) one brother's books — two brothers' books
   b) one child's tent — four children's tents
   c) one pupil's pen — ten pupils' pens

Seite 81

2.

	R	F
a) The front of the house.	☑	☐
b) The shoe's colour.	☐	☑
c) The girl's smile.	☑	☐

3. the candles of the cake
   the leaves of the tree
   the surprise of the day
   the size of the present

4. a) King Arthur's knights sat around a round table.
   b) The colour of the table was gold.
   c) The queen's dress was silver.
   d) The size of the castle was huge.
   e) The black prince was the people's fear.

5. a) Family Jones' holidays were terrible.
   b) The colour of the new car is terrible.
   c) The children's presents were expensive.
   d) The cats' eyes were green.

Seite 82

6. The boy's bag.
   The pupils' lesson.
   The children's holidays.
   The map of Germany.
   The girls' textbook.

7. a) The queen's dress was beautiful.
   b) The king's eyes were closed.
   c) The men's laughter was loud.

Seite 83

Test

1. a) The ladies' dresses looked lovely.
   b) The gardens of the castle were beautiful.
   c) The prince's eyes were shining when he saw the lady.

2. a) My parents' car is new.
   b) The pupil's new uniform looks good.
   c) The windows of the old house were broken.

3. a) the page of the book
   b) Linda's dog
   c) teacher's bag
   d) the sole of the shoes

Nomen

Auswertung zum Test
Ziehe dir für jeden Fehler einen Punkt ab.

Von insgesamt 10 Punkten hast du .... Punkte erreicht.

Super!	In Ordnung!	Bitte noch einmal üben!
10 bis 9 Punkte	8 bis 6 Punkte	Weniger als 6 Punkte

Seite 84

1. a) Becky's two dogs are crazy.
   b) The Burtons' children are nice.
   c) Are the children's bags in the classroom?
   d) Lars' teacher is very nice.

2. Maggy is on a school exchange visit in England. Her suitcases have not arrived so far. She is very upset. Agnes, her English host sister, offers Maggy some of her own clothes. Agnes' clothes are quite trendy and Maggy likes them. Yesterday they went to Madame Susanne's, a new hairstyling salon in London. Agnes and Maggy's hair is now pink and very spiky. Maggy's mother saw it on Skype and could not stop laughing. She kept saying: "Oh my God!"

Seite 85

3. a) I am going to the doctor's.
   b) Uncle Jerry and Aunt Joy's last holidays were terrible.

Test

1. a) I am not feeling well. Let's go to ☑ the doctor's. ☐ doctors.
   b) ☐ "Car's" ☑ "Cars" is the name of a kids movie.
   c) It's raining ☐ cat and dog's ☑ cats and dogs.
   d) ☑ Becky and James' ☐ Becky's and James's holidays were really good.

2. a) Anna is at her grandparents'.
   b) William and Harold's soldiers fought a terrible battle.
   c) Louis' sword was very old.

Auswertung zum Test
Ziehe dir für jeden Fehler einen Punkt ab.

Von insgesamt 7 Punkten hast du .... Punkte erreicht.

Super!	In Ordnung!	Bitte noch einmal üben!
7 Punkte	6 bis 5 Punkte	Weniger als 5 Punkte

Seite 86

1.

zählbar	***nicht zählbar***
apples cakes oranges eggs games dolls cars songs books clouds snowflakes frogs umbrellas	milk sugar juice fun music rain sunshine ice

Seite 87

2. Individuelle Lösung. Du musst bei deinen Sätzen folgende Kombinationen verwendet haben.
   – much milk, much sugar, much juice, much fun, much music, much rain, much sunshine, much ice
   – many apples, many cakes, many oranges, many eggs, many games, many dolls, many cars, many songs, many books, many clouds, many snowflakes, many frogs, many umbrellas

3. a) There isn't much milk left, Sarah. No, but we have a lot of apple juice.
   b) How much time do you need?
   c) Oh, you have got so many rabbits!

4. a) You have got many books!
   b) I don't have so much time.
   c) You are allowed to make a lot of noise.

Test
   a) Thank you very much.
   b) How many doggy biscuits are left?
   c) We have lots of very nice girls in our class.
   d) You have so many nice flowers in your garden!

Auswertung zum Test
Ziehe dir für jeden Fehler einen Punkt ab.

Von insgesamt 4 Punkten hast du .... Punkte erreicht.

Super!	In Ordnung!	Bitte noch einmal üben!
4 Punkte	3 Punkte	Weniger als 3 Punkte

Seite 88

1. a) I would like ☑ some ☐ any extra jam, please.
   b) I don't have ☐ some ☑ any French fries!
   c) Are there ☐ some ☑ any sweets left?

2. a) Have you ever seen any ghosts?
   b) Yes, I saw some when we went to Scotland last year.
   c) Could you tell me any stories about ghosts?
   e) I think there are no ghosts.

Seite 89

3. a) Is there anybody out there?
   b) I can see something!
   c) Could you do something for me, please?

Nomen

Test

Sherlock Holmes waited outside. “Can you see anything, Watson?“
“No, I can’t. It’s too dark to see a person!” They waited. Suddenly they heard something. Was it the thief? They needed some candles. Watson didn’t have any, but Sherlock Holmes found matches and a candle in his coat. “Somebody must stop this thief!” said Watson, “Isn’t there anything we can do?” “There is always somebody who can do the right thing!” said Sherlock Holmes.

Auswertung zum Test

Gib dir für jede richtig gefüllte Lücke einen Punkt.

Von insgesamt 7 Punkten hast du …….. Punkte erreicht.

Super!	In Ordnung!	Bitte noch einmal üben!
7 Punkte	6 bis 5 Punkte	Weniger als 5 Punkte

Seite 90

1.

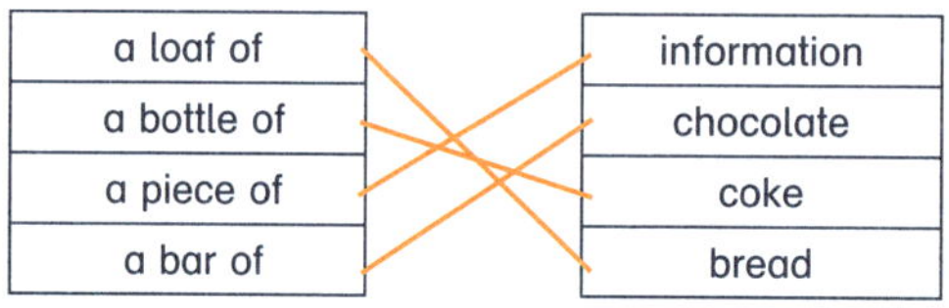

Seite 91

2. a) Do you have a pen for me? – No, but you can have a pencil.
   b) Would you like a bar of chocolate?

3. a) I like this piece of furniture.
   b) I need to buy three bottles of water.

4. a) Would you please give me a bottle of/a glass of milk.
   b) I need information.
   c) There is a cup of tea waiting for you.

Test

1. Airline Staff: “Good morning, Sir. How many pieces of luggage are you checking in?” You: “Three. How many bottles of water may I take with me?” Airline staff: “None. Sorry, Sir.” You: “Oh. But I may take my bar of chocolate, right?” Airline staff: “That is no problem, Sir.”

2. a) Anna is writing a letter to her exchange student.
   b) I would like to drink a cup of coffee.
   c) Edmund would never drink a bottle of/a glass of coke.

Auswertung zum Test

Bei Aufgabe 1 bekommst du für jede richtig gefüllte Lücke einen Punkt. Bei Aufgabe 2 ist jede Teilaufgabe einen Punkt wert.

Von insgesamt 6 Punkten hast du …….. Punkte erreicht.

Super!	In Ordnung!	Bitte noch einmal üben!
6 Punkte	5 bis 4 Punkte	Weniger als 4 Punkte

Kapitel 4: Pronomen

Seite 92

1. a) She is a nice girl.
   b) It is very big.
   c) They are brothers.
   d) He is never here.

Seite 93

2. a) She gave it to her.
   b) Give me my glasses, please!
   c) We like them.

3. a) This is his cat.
   b) Where are my shoes?
   c) These are her skates.
   d) This is their problem.

4. a) We are early.
   b) I am from Germany.
   c) They play football. They are playing football.

Seite 94

5.

a)	Is this	☐ you're	☒ your	bag?
b)	☒ It's	☐ its		warm today.
c)	☒ Their	☐ They'r		car is new.

6.

	R	F	
a) Can you see Rashid? I can't see him.	☑	☐	
b) See your later!	☐	☑	Korrekt: See you later!
c) Give him his book, please.	☑	☐	
d) Can you help my?	☐	☑	Korrekt: Can you help me?

7. One day the young girl, Molly, wanted to go to town. Her father had told her not to go out alone. But he was not at home, so Molly decided to go. She put on her best dress and left the house. It was a long way and Molly became tired. She went to sleep under a big tree. When she woke up there was golden sand under her feet and she could hear lovely music. "Where am I?" And then she heard the most beautiful voice. It whispered the secret message.

Seite 95

Test

1. a) This is her new dress.
   b) Just look at her! She looks lovely.
   c) Jason thinks she looks lovely, too.
   d) What do you think, Finn?

2. a) Our house is green.
   b) We love chocolate ice cream.
   c) You/I don't like spiders.

3. a) This is not your problem!
   b) I like your new hairstyle.
   c) It's very cold today!
   d) The river is fast. Its water is very cold.

Auswertung zum Test
Für jede richtig gelöste Teilaufgabe bekommst du einen Punkt.

Von insgesamt 11 Punkten hast du .... Punkte erreicht.

Super!	In Ordnung!	Bitte noch einmal üben!
11 bis 10 Punkte	9 bis 7 Punkte	Weniger als 7 Punkte

Seite 96

1. a) Oh, is that Nadja's notebook? Yes, that is hers.
   b) Is that my problem or Anna and Ben's problem? No, it is theirs.
   c) Hey, I know Andy, too. Is he a friend of yours?

Seite 97

2. a) Is this my seat/place? Yes, it is yours.
   b) Ronja and Toni are friends of ours.
   c) Whose books are these? These are ours.

3.

meins	mine	mein	my
deins	yours	dein	your
Seins/ihrs/ seins	his/hers/its	sein/ihr/sein	his/her/its
unseres	ours	unser	our
eu[e]res	yours	euer	your
ihres	theirs	ihr	their

Test

1. a) Whose dirty socks are these? They are not mine.
   b) Their answers are very good.
   c) The dog is huge. Its paws are as big as my hand!

2. a) Sheila and Anton are friends of his.
   b) Your coat is here, but mine is not.

Auswertung zum Test
Ziehe dir für jeden Fehler einen Punkt ab.

Von insgesamt 5 Punkten hast du .... Punkte erreicht.

Super!	In Ordnung!	Bitte noch einmal üben!
5 Punkte	4 Punkte	Weniger als 4 Punkte

Seite 98

1. a) I look at myself in the mirror.
   b) Ben always thinks of himself first.
   c) She has hurt herself.
   d) Let's take photos of ourselves.

Seite 99

2. a) Tom, you knew yourself that it was stupid to drive dad's new car.
   b) You have created a big problem yourself.
   c) Dad himself said that the repairs will be expensive!
   d) I have never done something like that myself.

3. a) Try to remember.
   b) Listen to yourself.
   c) I feel good.

4. a) She never liked herself.
   b) They looked at each other and laughed.
   c) Try to remember!
   d) Grandmother herself told me the story.

Seite 100

5. a) We felt good.
   b) It moved very slowly.
   c) Don't hurt yourself.

6. a) The forrest can't destroy itself.
   b) They were laughing about themselves.
   c) I was shocked about myself.
   d) We have never locked ourselves out before.
   d) Benjam and Franklin! Just look at yourselves.

Seite 101

Test

Hello Rashid,

I must tell you what happened last week. My sister and I went camping on our own. I like to put the tent up myself, because Jill often makes a mess of it. She herself says that she is not good at it. Tsts, girls! Anyway, we were out in the wild, listening to ourselves sing and feeling good. Suddenly there was a really funny noise. Jill and I looked at each other. We immediately thought: BEAR! The bears in Maine are not big, but you don't want to meet one. We told each other to keep cool and I decided to have a look. I walked over to some bushes and then I found myself looking at some very long legs. I looked up and the owner of the legs looked down. We stared at each other for at least a minute before the moose snorted, scratched itself and left. Boy, I was happy about meeting a moose and not a bear. How are your holidays? Have you had any adventures yourself?

Yours Finn

Auswertung zum Test

Ziehe dir für jeden Fehler einen Punkt ab.

Von insgesamt 13 Punkten hast du .... Punkte erreicht.

Super!	In Ordnung!	Bitte noch einmal üben!
13 bis 11 Punkte	10 bis 8 Punkte	Weniger als 8 Punkte

Kapitel 5: Artikel

Seite 102

1. a) Could you pass me an apple?
   b) This is a nice class.
   c) We have to wait an hour.

Seite 103

2. a) Yesterday I saw an elephant.
   b) Today I want to see a monkey.

3. a) When does school begin in England?
   b) The family has dinner at eight.
   c) We all like to go outside because we really love nature.
   d) Did you see tigers when you lived in India?

4. a) I go to school every day.
   b) I eat a banana every day.
   c) I love horses.

5.

		R	F	
a)	Pass me a orange, please.	☐	☑	Korrekt: Pass me an orange, please.
b)	Where is the train station?	☑	☐	
c)	I don't like the Mondays.	☐	☑	Korrekt: I don't like Mondays.

Seite 104

6. a) an old man
   b) a pretty girl
   c) a dangerous bus stop
   d) an interesting story
   e) an exciting holiday

7. Beispiellösungen
   a) My grandfather is an old man.
   b) Angelina is a pretty girl.
   c) This is a dangerous bus stop.
   d) I heard an interesting story yesterday.
   e) We had an exciting holiday

Seite 105

Test

1. a) Do you like the show?
   b) I live in an old house.
   c) My grandparents have hens and goats.
   d) Would you like to have dinner with me?

2. a) Our class has a nice teacher.
   b) Pupils like to talk.

3. a) She lives in a very old house.
   b) They live in an old house, too.
   c) I love nature. (Hier darf kein Artikel gesetzt werden)
   d) Don't forget to take an umbrella.
   e) We can't see the road!

Auswertung zum Test
Ziehe dir für jeden Fehler einen Punkt ab.

Von insgesamt 12 Punkten hast du .... Punkte erreicht.

Super!	In Ordnung!	Bitte noch einmal üben!
12 bis 11 Punkte	10 bis 7 Punkte	Weniger als 7 Punkte

Kapitel 6: Adjektive und Adverbien

1. a) nicely   d) newly   Seite 106
   b) loudly   e) badly
   c) well   f) awfully

2. Seite 107

		R	F	
a)	She called out loud.	☐	☑	Korrekt: She called out loudly.
b)	Please walk slowly!	☑	☐	
c)	That was good done!	☐	☑	Korrekt: That was well done.

3. a) I am a good tennis player.
   b) Lynn can sing beautifully.
   c) We work very hard.
   d) Please carry the bowl carefully.

4. a) Benjamin sings beautifully.
   b) I can cut hair well.

5. a) The baby cries loudly.
   b) The dog is happy.

6. This is Anna's family. Her sister Leni is 18 years old and she is very beautiful. Leni can dance very well. Mina is the middle sister. She loves to cook and she can taste very well. She wants to have her own restaurant and create her own food. Her cakes are always fantastic. Anna's parents love dogs, so the family has a dog, Nelly. Nelly is a very happy dog. When Anna throws a ball she runs after it happily. They all live in an old house. Seite 108

7. a) Linda has a new dress. It looks good. Seite 109
   b) I can smell very well.
   c) The pullover doesn't smell good.

8. Adjektive beschreiben, wie jemand oder etwas ist.
   Adverbien beschreiben, wie jemand etwas tut.

9. a) Jamie Oliver is a good cook. He cooks well.
   b) Anna is a fast learner. She always learns fast.

10. a) Does the bird sing loudly?
    b) Could you please practice your vocabulary quietly?
    c) Does the pizza taste good?

Seite 110

11. We were very happy. The Christmas holiday had started and we were on our way home. Only Jane felt sad. "Is the new house nice?" she asked nervously. "I really liked our old house. I don't want to live in a new house." she told me. I put my arm around her lovingly and gave her my best smile. "It is wonderful, Jane. From your room you can see the sea and the beach." Her parents had decorated her room prettily with seashells and little boats.

12. a) They laughed nervously
    b) You have a loud voice.
    c) The never do things nicely.

Seite 111

Test

1. a) John sings ~~beautiful~~/**beautifully**.
   b) Anna was very ill. Today she looks ~~good~~/**well**.
   c) He listens ~~carful~~/**carefully**.
   d) That birthday party was **good**/~~well~~.

2. a) Our teacher is nice. She always treats us nicely.
   b) Kevin is a slow writer. He writes slowly.

3. a) Ben works hard.
   b) I am a good football player.
   c) Your father/My father can cook well.
   d) Your friend/My friend looks good.

Auswertung zum Test
Für jede richtig gelöste Teilaufgabe bekommst du einen Punkt.

Von insgesamt 10 Punkten hast du .... Punkte erreicht.

Super!	In Ordnung!	Bitte noch einmal üben!
10 bis 9 Punkte	8 bis 6 Punkte	Weniger als 6 Punkte

Seite 112

1. a) high higher highest
   b) big bigger biggest
   c) little less least
   d) terrible more terrible most terrible
   e) bad worse worst

2. a) Lynn sings beautifully. Yes, but Anna sings more beautifully. But Ronja sings the most beautifully. Seite 113
   b) Toni runs fast. Ben runs faster. But Dave runs fastest.
   c) That was bad news. This is worse news. Let's hope there will not be the worst news.

3. terrible more terrible most terrible
   good better best
   nice nicer nicest
   clear clearer clearest
   little less least
   slow slower slowest

4. a) My test is better.
   b) This was the best party.
   c) Luka got the most presents.

5. a) James is the fastest runner at our school. Seite 114
   b) Jenny is a better dancer than Betty.
   c) Ann was a famous queen, but Elizabeth I was the most famous queen of England.
   d) Archibald is the biggest dog I have ever seen!

6. a) A mouse is smaller than a rat.
   b) That was the most dangerous thing I have ever done.
   c) Being thirsty is worse than being hungry.

7. a) Is the cake sweeter than the ice cream?
   b) Is the queen more beautiful than the princess?
   c) Is the elephant the strongest animal?

Test Seite 115

1. a) "The never ending story" is a wonderful book.
   b) The experiment is more interesting than the text.
   c) I ate the best ice cream in town.

2. a) I had the worst dream!
   b) Who is the nicest girl?
   c) That dog is smaller than my cat.

3. a) Your English is not bad.
   b) They have the best pizza in town.

Auswertung zum Test

Ziehe dir für jeden Fehler einen Punkt ab.

Von insgesamt 8 Punkten hast du .... Punkte erreicht.

Super!	In Ordnung!	Bitte noch einmal üben!
8 bis 7 Punkte	6 bis 5 Punkte	Weniger als 5 Punkte

Adjektive und Adverbien

Seite 116

1. a) A mountain is higher than a hill.
   b) A river is wider than a stream.
   c) A pony is smaller than a horse.

2. a) Lynn is as tall as Leni.
   b) Lynn's hair is as long as Leni's hair.
   c) Lynn's voice is as strong as Leni's voice.
   d) Lynn talks as much as Leni.

Seite 117

3. a) A smartphone is as expensive as a camera.
   b) Chinese is more difficult than English.
   c) Germany is not as hot as Australia.

4. a) I run faster than my friend.
   b) My mother cooks as well as my father.
   c) My English is better than my French.

5. a) This is worse than I thought.
   b) My present is as big as yours.

Seite 118

6. a) Sam is tall. Stan is not as tall as Sam.
   b) Sam is good at Math. Stan is not as good at Math as Sam.
   c) Sam is a good dancer. Stan is a better dancer than Sam.

7. a) Do I cook better than I sing?
   b) Are my holidays longer than yours?
   c) Is the film as good as the book?

8. Dear Grandma,
   We have finally arrived in Arizona. The countryside is more interesting than you can imagine! The weather here is awesome – although it is not as hot as I thought. Many people run around wearing real cowboy hats which I find very cool. They are much cooler than the people at home. I'll write again soon and send a picture with me and my new hat!
   Yours Dylan

Seite 119

Test

1. a) This holiday was better than the last.
   b) Megan is as sad as Tom.
   c) Sunday is not as bad as Monday.

2. a) That film is as god as this film.
   b) This song is better than that song.
   c) This book is more interesting than that book.
   d) This hobby is as dangerous as that hobby

Auswertung zum Test

Alles richtig? Dann hast du 7 Punkte. Ziehe dir für jeden Fehler einen Punkt ab.

Von insgesamt 7 Punkten hast du .... Punkte erreicht.

Super!	In Ordnung!	Bitte noch einmal üben!
7 Punkte	6 bis 5 Punkte	Weniger als 5 Punkte

Kapitel 7: Adverbien

1. a) You are always dreaming. Seite 120
   b) We often go swimming.
   c) Becky is always late.
   d) Max never shouts.

2. a) Anna is usually very friendly. Seite 121
   b) I always go for a walk.
   c) My dog sometimes barks.
   d) Do you often jog?

3. a) I visit my grandmother regularly.
   b) We seldom get homework on Friday.
   c) Layla often feels bored.

4. Häufigkeitsadverbien stehen vor dem Vollverb. Wenn aber eine Form von to be im Satz steht, so stehen die Häufigkeitsadverbien nach der Form von to be.

5. Seite 122

Q	W	E	R	T	Z	U	I	O
S	A	L	W	A	Y	S	P	F
R	I	P	L	C	Y	U	L	T
N	E	V	E	R	A	A	K	E
T	Y	V	M	V	S	L	H	N
N	N	O	R	M	A	L	L	Y
T	M	R	N	B	D	Y	G	F
S	O	M	E	T	I	M	E	S

6. a) I never come home late.
   b) We go to the theatre regularly.
   c) She doesn't visit her grandmother often.
   d) I normally don't sleep late. / I don't sleep late normally.

7. a) often/regularly/normally/~~never~~
   b) seldom/occasionally/sometimes/~~usually~~

Adverbien

Seite 123 Test

1. a) My brother is seldom angry. / My brother seldom gets upset.
   b) Usually she gets up late.
   c) I often listen to the radio.

2. a) My father takes milk in his tea sometimes. Sometimes my father takes milk in his tea.
   b) I usually do my homework.
   c) We go to the gym regularly.

3. a) I **sometimes/~~never~~** go to the gym, but I should go more often.
   b) Do you visit your cousin in the States **regularly/~~usually~~**?
   c) They are **always/~~occasionally~~** late. It drives me crazy!

Auswertung zum Test
Ziehe dir für jeden Fehler ein Punkt ab.

Von insgesamt 9 Punkten hast du .... Punkte erreicht.

Super!	In Ordnung!	Bitte noch einmal üben!
9 bis 8 Punkte	7 bis 6 Punkte	Weniger als 6 Punkte

Seite 124

1. a) Zoe always goes to see movies at the weekend.
   b) She never comes home on time.
   c) Of course her mother is upset.
   d) Zoe is tired because she hardly sleeps enough.

Seite 125

2. a) I usually meet my friends on Saturday.
   b) This sounds like a good idea.
   c) Suddenly I had a terrible headache.
   d) She almost had an accident.

3. a) James doesn't play football well.
   b) The children became hungry.
   c) That was quite dangerous!
   d) Unfortunately I can't come.

Seite 126

4. a) Why are you always **late/~~lately~~**, Zoe?
   b) What is so **terrible/~~terribly~~** about being late, Mum?
   c) She does her work **~~careful~~/carefully**.
   d) This pizza smells **good/~~well~~**!

5. a) Most sportsmen play fair.
   b) Anna bakes well.
   c) Luka drives well.
   d) I read fast.

6. For many people London is one the most exciting cities. People from all over the world come to see its fascinating historic sights. It's hardly possible to see everything in one visit. There are nearly 5000 overseas banks in the financial centre of the city, so London is an important European business centre.

Test

Seite 127

1. a) I can smell well.
   b) The weather changes quickly here.
   c) I don't feel well. /I feel ill.

2. a) I will never see you again!
   b) The keys are here!
   c) Maybe we can wait and see?

3. a) She walks around ☐ slow ☒ slowly.
   b) He is very ☒ careful ☐ carefully.

4. a) Life is often surprising.
   b) He takes pictures well/very well.
   c) Zoe lies badly.

Auswertung zum Test
Du bekommst für jede richtig gelöste Teilaufgabe einen Punkt.

Von insgesamt 11 Punkten hast du .... Punkte erreicht.

Super!	In Ordnung!	Bitte noch einmal üben!
11 bis 10 Punkte	9 bis 7 Punkte	Weniger als 7 Punkte

Kapitel 8: Satzbau

Seite 129

1. a) My family lives in an old house.
   b) Where are you?
   c) We eat pizza every weekend.

2. a) She listens to the radio every morning.
   b) They share secrets at night.
   c) He visits his grandparents every day.

3. a) What do you eat in the morning?
   b) Where does she live?
   c) Who is the new girl.

Seite 130

4. a) My father is in the garden.
   b) My father reads the newspaper every morning.
   c) My father watches the news every evening.

5. Der Satzbau in Aussagesätzen sieht so aus: Subjekt, Prädikat, Objekt, Ort und Zeit.
Bei Fragesätzen mit Vollverb steht erst das Fragewort, es folgen do/does/did und dann Subjekt und Verb.
Ist ein Hilfsverb im Satz, sieht der Satzbau so aus: Fragewort, Hilfsverb, Subjekt und Verb.

Seite 131

6. a) I am doing my homework at the moment.
   b) Open the window.
   c) Never do that.

Test

1. a) The flowers smell lovely in the afternoon.
   b) The old house looks very scary at night.
   c) I feel sleepy in the morning.

2. a) I live in a small town in Germany.
   b) We wanted to go swimming this morning.
   c) The dog walks down the street every evening.

Auswertung zum Test

Ziehe dir für jeden Fehler einen Punkt ab.

Von insgesamt 6 Punkten hast du …….. Punkte erreicht.

Super!	In Ordnung!	Bitte noch einmal üben!
6 Punkte	5 bis 4 Punkte	Weniger als 4 Punkte

Kapitel 9: If-Sätze

Seite 133

1. a) If you call me, I will tell you the story.
   b) She will buy the dress if she has enough money.
   c) We will not come if you don't ask us.

2. a) ☐ If ☒ When we have the new car, we will go for a drive.
   b) ☒ If ☐ When you are late again, mum will be angry!

3. a) I will not be allowed to go to the party if I don't tidy my room.
   b) My family will fly to Paris when it is my aunt's birthday.
   c) Ben will be happy if Anna really calls.

4. a) If I don't do my homework, I will not go out.
   b) If you use less salt, the food will taste better.

Seite 134

5. a) My brother will miss the train if he doesn't hurry.
   b) My sister will buy the red shoes if she has enough money.
   c) If my father likes the black jeep, he will buy it.
   d) If my mother finishes her Italian class, she will travel to Italy.

6 a) If Sam helps David, he will be faster.
b) If you go to bed so late, you will be tired.
c) If a lion is hungry, he will hunt for food.
d) If the pupils have enough time, they will go to the beach.
e) If it snows, I will build a snowman.

Test

Seite 135

1. a) I will catch the bus if I hurry.
b) Anna will go to dinner with Tom if he asks her.

2. a) They won't be quiet if there is so much noise outside.
b) He will win the match if he plays like this.

3. a) I will learn how to drive when I am 18.
b) Tom will buy a house in Spain if he earns a lot of money./Tom will earn a lot of money if he buys a house in Spain.

Auswertung zum Test

Gib dir für jede richtig gelöste Teilaufgabe einen Punkt.

Von insgesamt 6 Punkten hast du .... Punkte erreicht.

Super!	In Ordnung!	Bitte noch einmal üben!
6 Punkte	5 bis 4 Punkte	Weniger als 4 Punkte

Seite 136

1.

… the cat (to cross) the road …	… we (to save) the planet.
… we (to run) fast enough …	… we (to catch) the bus.
… all of us (to help) …	… it (to be) in great danger.

If the cat crossed the road, it would be in great danger.
If we ran fast enough, we would catch the bus.
If all of us helped, we could save the planet.

2. a) My test would be better if I studied more.
b) You wouldn't be so tired if you went to bed earlier.
c) If he had her mobile number, he would call her.

Seite 137

3. Have you ever been to the rainforest? The biggest rainforest is in Brazil. It is on the Amazon river and you have probably heard about it. It is in great danger. If we don't stop to cut down the forest, there will not be any rainforest left in 100 years. But why do people of big companies do that? They want more grazing land for their cows so they can sell more meat to fast food restaurants or meat factories. But if the rainforest disappears, millions of animals will die. If we burn more trees there every day, the weather will change and it will get warmer. If there is no more rainforest to filter the air, it won't be clean anymore.

4. a) My test would have been better if I had studied more.
   b) My friend will hurt himself if he drives so fast.
   c) I would not have got so wet if I had taken an umbrella.
   d) It would not be so bad if it didn't hurt so much.

Seite 138

5. a) Typ 3 b) Typ 2 c) Typ 3

6. a) If it had never happened, they would have been happy.
   b) She wouldn't have this problem if she had been faster.

Seite 139

Test

1. a) I would open the door if I hadn't lost the keys.
   b) If my brother hadn't left, he would not have been on time.
   c) My teacher would do corrections faster if he had more time.

2. a) If we had known, we would have helped you.
   b) I would have gone to the concert if I had had the money for the ticket.
   c) If he hadn't eaten so much cake at the party, he would not have felt sick later.

Auswertung zum Test

Gib dir bei Aufgabe 1 für jede richtige Teillösung zwei Punkte und bei Aufgabe 2 für jede richtig gefüllte Lücke einen Punkt.

Von insgesamt 12 Punkten hast du .... Punkte erreicht.

Super!	In Ordnung!	Bitte noch einmal üben!
12 bis 11 Punkte	10 bis 7 Punkte	Weniger als 7 Punkte

Kapitel 10: Relativsätze

Seite 140

1. a) This is the program about the rainforest which I saw yesterday.
   b) There was a man who lives in the rainforest.
   c) He lives there with the Kayapo, who are an Indian tribe.

Seite 141

2. a) Benjamin is a boy who loves sports.
   b) "This is the hairstyle which I want to have."
   c) Where are the people who asked for me?

3. a) Can you see the tiger which is jumping over the burning fence?
   b) My favorite book is a fairytale book that my mum always read to me.
   c) All the students who forgot their homework have to come to the front.

4. a) This book, which I love, is about a big adventure.
   b) There is the bus which I just missed.
   c) I have a music CD which is really good.

5. a) Do you know the girl who is standing in the corner?
   b) The dogs which/that look like lions are my favourite.
   c) Where is the boy who broke his arm last week?

6. | | mit | ohne
--- | --- | ---
a) This is a frog which is very toxic (giftig). | ☑ | ☐
b) This is the window (that) I cleaned yesterday. | ☐ | ☑
c) A Kapayo is a person who lives in the rainforest. | ☑ | ☐
d) This was the TV program (which) I saw yesterday. | ☐ | ☑

Seite 142

7. a) Many years ago, I went to the rainforest which is on the Amazonas.
   b) There were many plants that I had never seen before.
   c) There were also some animals which looked very strange.

8. a) This ist he girl who has such a lovely voice.
   b) I like the movie I saw yesterday.
   c) Who knows the song about the rainforest?
   d) Have you got the present I bought for you?

9. a) Anna started a campaign that helps to protect the rainforest.
   b) The red-eyed frog is in the book which I bought last week.
   c) The meat that the fast food restaurants sell is part of the problem.

Seite 143

10. a) The scientist who discovered a new planet has won the Nobel Prize.
    b) The student who took drugs had to leave school.
    c) The little girl who had been lost in a National Park has been found.

Seite 144

11. a) The girl who paid for the ice cream is Mary's friend.
    b) From here you can see the mountain that we climbed.
    c) The detective lost the man who/that he was following.
    d) The pony that/which I used to ride is very old now.

Test

Seite 145

1. a) Basketball is a game which/that is fast.
   b) Mrs Little is the teacher who teaches maths.
   c) France is a country which/that is famous for food and wine.

2. a) This is my grandmother Iris who lives in India.
   b) India is a big country which fascinates many people.
   c) There are many interesting places that are beautiful.

3. a) The rainforest tribes are people who live in the rainforest.
   b) To protect the rainforest area, which they live in, is a very important goal.

Auswertung zum Test

Du bekommst für jede richtig gelöste Teilaufgabe einen Punkt.

Von insgesamt 8 Punkten hast du .... Punkte erreicht.

Super!	In Ordnung!	Bitte noch einmal üben!
8 bis 7 Punkte	6 bis 5 Punkte	Weniger als 5 Punkte

Seite 146

1. a) I will bring whatever my family needs.
   b) It was not where it should be.

2. a) I can leave whenever you are ready.
   b) What made me nervous was their idea of having fun.

3. a) Most of the songs which we listened to were very good.
   b) This is the decision that we came to.

Seite 147

4. a) I need an idea that will save me. Freier Relativsatz ☐
   b) They did what they wanted. Freier Relativsatz ☑

Test

1. a) Whoever sent Anna those/the flowers made her smile.
   b) Anna loves what she hears.
   c) She went wherever the wind carried her.

2. a) The girl with the long black hair is the one who he danced with.
   b) The party which we went to was very good.
   c) Most of the girls that he danced with were not as pretty.

Auswertung zum Test

Für jede richtig gelöste Teilaufgabe bekommst du einen Punkt.

Von insgesamt 6 Punkten hast du .... Punkte erreicht.

Super!	In Ordnung!	Bitte noch einmal üben!
6 Punkte	5 bis 4 Punkte	Weniger als 4 Punkte

Kapitel 11: Konjunktionen

Seite 148

1. a) I have four sisters and four brothers, and we all live together in a very big house.
   b) She doesn't want to eat the cake, because she doesn't like strawberries.
   c) We could watch a movie, or we could go outside.

2. a) Hannah has a cold so she won't go to the beach today.
   b) Jessy knows many things but she doesn't know the answer to that question.
   c) Ben's team is very good because they work very hard.

3. a) I don't go to school today, because I am ill.
   b) Tom can watch a movie or meet Ben.

Seite 149

4. One evening I was alone at home and Mum told me to read a nice book. She told me to go to bed early but I watched a scary movie. Suddenly I heard a sound outside so I went to the window but it was dark. I could not see anything. I quickly hid behind the sofa because I was very scared. Then I heard my father's voice: "Benjam Thomas Miller! Where are you and why is the TV on?" I was happy to hear my father's voice.

Test

1. a) I don't have any homework, so I can meet my friends this afternoon.
   b) We will go to the movies, and then we can go and have dinner somewhere.
   c) Would you like a sausage, or do you prefer a steak?

2. a) My mother will come home late tonight, because she has to work longer.
   b) The telephone rang so I answered it.

Auswertung zum Test

Bei Aufgabe 1 bekommst du für jedes richtig eingesetzte Wort einen Punkt. Bei Aufgabe 2 ist jede Teilaufgabe zwei Punkte wert.

Von insgesamt 7 Punkten hast du .... Punkte erreicht.

Super!	In Ordnung!	Bitte noch einmal üben!
7 Punkte	6 bis 5 Punkte	Weniger als 5 Punkte

Seite 150

1. a) Two days ago, when the weather was great, my Grandpa and I climbed up a hill.
   b) When we reached the top of the hill I looked up at the sky and saw black clouds.
   c) Because of the strong rain I could not see but I think there was a lonely figure standing on a rock.

2. a) When the rain stopped, the figure was gone.
   b) Because I wanted to know who the man was, I asked an old lady.
   c) She said that he was a ghost and because of a lost love he always came out in the rain.

Seite 151

3. a) I could not see because of the rain.
   b) The man stood in the rain because of a lost love.
   c) When it stopped raining, the sun was shining.

4. Beispiellösung
   a) Because of you I came too late.
   b) I could not come home earlier because I missed the bus.
   c) When my mum makes pizza, I am always home on time.

Seite 152

5. a) I love Christmas because my whole family will be home.
   b) Because the weather was bad we went home.
   c) When Anna visits me tomorrow, we will go to the beach.

6. a) When he said, that I was wrong I became angry.
   b) I never eat seafood because I don't like the taste.
   c) I was happy because of the lovely surprise.

7. a) Was she late because of me?
   b) Did he forget the book because he was in a hurry?

Konjunktionen

Seite 153

Test

1. a) When he saw the man in the rain, Ben immediately told his grandfather.
   b) When Ben came home, he told his sister the story.
   c) Because Anne doesn't believe in ghosts, she did not believe Ben.

2. a) I had to laugh because of you.
   b) I have to go home, because it is late.
   c) I went to sleep when it became dark.

3. a) I did this because of you.
   b) When she finds out, she will be angry.
   c) We didn't buy any nuts, because of my allergy.

Auswertung zum Test

Gib dir für jede richtig gelöste Teilaufgabe einen Punkt.

Von insgesamt 9 Punkten hast du .... Punkte erreicht.

Super!	In Ordnung!	Bitte noch einmal üben!
9 bis 8 Punkte	7 bis 6 Punkte	Weniger als 6 Punkte

Seite 154

1. a) We waited until it was dark.
   b) My brother wants to be a firefighter when he grows up.
   c) Becka came to school, although she was not feeling well.

2. a) I went to see that movie, although I am scared of wolves.
   b) I won't go to the beach if I don't feel better.
   c) You should think before you speak.

Seite 155

3. a) It was calm after the storm.
   b) I will fly to America, although I am afraid of flying.
   c) I will fly to America, because my best friend lives there.

4.

	R	F
a) Since we are here anyway, we can enjoy it.	☑	☐
b) When you like, we can go to Edinburgh.	☐	☑
c) I want to go to the Festival because it is famous.	☑	☐

5. It was dark. Although they couldn't see anything, the five friends quietly moved forward. They would not leave the island until they had found out about its secret. "Now that we are here, we need a plan!" said George. In order to solve the mystery of the missing artifacts they had traveled far from home. "We should have thought of a plan before we came to a lonely island in the middle of the night!" grumbled Dick. Whether or not they liked it, they did not have a plan so far but there was somebody on this island who had a plan. And it wasn't for them. "We'll think of something. Hey, I know! Alright, come over here and listen." Anne always had the best ideas.

6. a) Do you want to eat pizza after the film? Seite 156
   b) Can I travel to America only if I have a passport?
   c) Do I need hiking boots in order to go on this trip?

Test

1. a) If you come home early, please make some tea .
   b) We can hire the bike for two weeks since/because it is very cheap.
   c) It is very cold although/even though the sun is shining.

2. Edinburgh has a long history because/as it is a very old city. Seite 157
   Before the Edinburgh Festival starts, thousands of people come to the city. Although/Even though not many people speak Gaelic, some of the plays at the Festival are in that old language. As/Since/Because the festival is now one of the most important festivals of music and drama, many people know about it. Since/Because/As the city is one of Europe's main cultural centres, there are many artists who live here.

3. a) I have been waiting since this morning.
   b) Because I read a fascinating story about it.
   c) I think I saw one, even if I don't believe in ghosts.

Auswertung zum Test

Bei den Aufgaben 1 und 3 bekommst du für jede richtig gelöste Teilaufgabe einen Punkt. Bei Aufgabe 2 bekommst du für jede richtig gefüllte Lücke einen Punkt.

Von insgesamt 11 Punkten hast du .... Punkte erreicht.

Super!	In Ordnung!	Bitte noch einmal üben!
11 bis 10 Punkte	9 bis 7 Punkte	Weniger als 7 Punkte

Glossar

Hier findest du wichtige Begriffe noch einmal erklärt.

- **Adjektive**: Adjektive beschreiben, wie jemand/ etwas ist.
- **adjective**, siehe Adjektive
- **Adverb**: Adverbien beschreiben, wie jemand etwas tut.
- **adverb**, siehe Adverb
- **Artikel** (engl. article): Es gibt bestimmte und unbestimmte Artikel. Sie begleiten Nomen. Im Englischen sind dies: **a**, **an** oder **the**.
- **article**, siehe Artikel
- **Bedingungssätze** (engl. conditional clauses): Sie drücken Bedingungen aus. **If he gets up early, he catches the train**.
- **conditional clauses**, siehe Bedingungssätze
- **contact clause:** Der contact clause ist ein Relativsatz ohne Relativpronomen. Man kann das Relativpronomen weglassen, wenn der Relativsatz ein notwendiger Relativsatz ist (siehe defining relative clause) und das Relativpronomen ein Objekt ersetzt. **The book I gave you was very old.**
- **coordinating conjunctions**, nebenordnende Konjunktionen: Sie haben die Aufgabe, Wörter, Wortgruppen oder ganze Sätze miteinander zu verbinden. **The pizza is hot and delicious**.
- **defining relative clause**: Relativsatz, der notwendig ist, um die Person oder die Sache zu definieren.
- **ever/never**: jemals/niemals, Signalwörter für present perfect
- **for**: seit (Zeitspanne), Signalwort für present perfect
- **Gegenwart**: Simple present, present progressive, present perfect sind Zeiten der Gegenwart.
- **Gerund**: Verb, das durch anhängen der -ing-Form als Nomen eingesetzt wird. **Reading is fun**.
- **Going-to-future**: eine Zeitform der Zukunft, die ein Vorhaben oder einen Plan ausdrückt

- **Hauptsatz:** Selbstständiger Satz. Ihm können Teilsätze untergeordnet sein.
- **Hilfsverb**: Die Hilfsverben to be, to do, to have werden benötigt, um andere grammatikalische Formen zu bilden (beispielsweise Verneinungen, manche Zeitformen)
- **If-Sätze**, siehe Bedingungssätze, conditional clauses
- **Infinitiv**: Grundform des Verbs (to play, to go, to sing), bei den unregelmäßigen Verben die erste der drei zu lernenden Formen
- **just**: gerade eben, Signalwort für present perfect
- **Konditionalsätze**, siehe Bedingungssätze
- **Konjunktionen**: Sie haben die Aufgabe, Wörter, Wortgruppen oder ganze Sätze miteinander zu verbinden. Siehe auch coordinating conjunctions. Häufige subordinating conjunctions sind: because, if, though, unless, where, while.
- **may**: vielleicht, möglicherweise, höfliche Form
- **Modalverben**: can, be able to, be allowed to, must, need, may. Verben, die Wunsch, Zwang oder Möglichkeit ausdrücken.
- **modal verbs**, siehe Modalverben
- **Nomen**: Hauptwort, Substantiv, Namenwort
- **nouns**, siehe Nomen: Diese werden im Englischen kleingeschrieben.
- **non defining relative clause**: Relativsatz, der nicht notwendige Zusatzinfomationen gibt, wird durch Komma vom übergeordneten Satz getrennt.
- **Objekt**: Satzergänzung. Die vom Subjekt ausgeführte Tätigkeit bezieht sich auf das Objekt. **He read the book**. book = Objekt.
- **object**, siehe Objekt
- **past progressive**: Verlaufsform der Vergangenheit. Eine Handlung, die zu einem bestimmten Zeitpunkt in der Vergangenheit gerade im Gange war.

- **past perfect**: Vorvergangenheit. Eine Handlung, die vor einer anderen Handlung in der Vergangenheit stattfand.
- **present progressive**: beschreibt Handlungen, die jetzt gerade stattfinden
- **present perfect**: Brücke zwischen Gegenwart und Vergangenheit. Für Handlungen, die angefangen aber noch nicht beendet sind, oder soeben beendet wurden, oder bei denen das Ergebnis im Vordergrund steht.
- **Pronomen**: ein Wort, das für ein Nomen eintritt (beispielsweise he statt Tom). **Tom is sick. He has got fever.**
- **pronoun**, siehe Pronomen
- **Relativpronomen**: Sie werden im Relativsatz benötigt, um einen Bezug herzustellen. **Do you see the dog which is chasing the rabbit?**
- **Relativsätze**: Relativsätze sind Attributsätze, also Nebensätze, die sich auf ein Nomen (oder Pronomen) im übergeordneten Satz (Hauptsatz) beziehen und dieses näher beschreiben. Siehe Beispielsatz bei Relativpronomen.
- **Satzstruktur**: Reihenfolge der Satzteile in Sätzen
- **Signalwörter**: Beispiele für Signalwörter sind: just, for/since, yesterday. Sie „signalisieren" etwa eine zu verwendende Zeitform.
- **simple past**: einfache Vergangenheit. Sie wird für Handlungen verwendet, die abgeschlossen sind.
- **simple present**: Zeitform der Gegenwart, die für regelmäßige Tätigkeiten und Fakten verwendet wird.
- **since** (seit, Zeitpunkt): Signalwort für present perfect, bezeichnet einen Zeitpunkt
- **unregelmäßige Verben**: Verben, die nicht mit -ed konjugiert werden. Es werden für unregelmäßige Verben immer drei Formen angeben: buy, bought, bought.
- **Vollverb**: Verb, das die Tätigkeit im Satz darstellt.
- **which**: Relativpronomen, für Dinge zu verwenden

- **who**: Relativpronomen, für Personen zu verwenden
- **will-future**: Zeitform der Zukunft
- **Zeitform**: Viele Sprachen unterscheiden drei als Tempora (Singular: Tempus) bezeichnet Zeitstufen: Vergangenheit, Gegenwart und Zukunft. Jedes Tempus wird durch Flexionsformen des Verbs dargestellt. Diese Flexionsformen nennt man Zeitformen.
- **Zeitpunkt**: wird im present perfect immer mit since eingeleitet
- **Zeitspanne**: wird im present perfect immer mit for eingeleitet

Stichwortverzeichnis

abstrakte Nomen 90
Adjektiv 62, 106
– Steigerung 112
Adverb 106, 120
adverbiale Bestimmung 124
after 46
and 148
any 88
Artikel 102
Aussagesatz 20, 26, 32, 36, 42, 46, 128
be 14, 15, 16
be able to 54
be allowed to 54
because 148, 150
because of 150
before 46
bestimmter Artikel 102
betonter Vokal 37
Bindewörter 148
but 148
can 50
can't 50
contact clause 146
coordinating conjunctions 148
defining relative clause 140
do 14, 16
each other 98
Eigennamen 84
einfache Vergangenheit 26
Endkonsonant 37
Ereignis 32, 46
for 66
Frage 20, 26, 32, 36, 42, 46
Fragesatz 128
Fragewort 16
Gegenwart 10, 20, 32
Genitiv 78, 80, 84
Gerund 60, 62
going-to-future 42
Großschreibung 70
Grundform 6, 50
Handlung 32, 46
Häufigkeitsadverb 120
Hauptsatz 132, 140
have 14, 16
have to 54
Hilfsverb 14, 15
how 16
if-clause 132, 136
If-Satz 132, 136
Imperativ 128
infinitive 6
Kleinschreibung 70
Konjunktion 150, 154
Konsonant 21
Konsonantenverdoppelung 6, 23
main clause 132
may 58
might 58
Modalverb 50, 54, 58
must 50
mustn't 50
Nebensatz 132
need 50
needn't 50
nicht zählbare Nomen 86, 90
no 88
non-defining relative clause 140
Nouns 70
Objekt 60
of-Genitiv 80
one 76
ones 76
or 148
Ortsangabe 66, 68

ought to 58
Passiv 14
past participle 6
past perfect 46
past progressive 36
Perfektform 14
Personalpronomen 92
Pluralform 72, 76
Possessivbegleiter 92, 96
Possessivpronomen 96
Präposition 62, 64, 68
Präsens 14
present perfect 32
present progressive 20, 23
pronouns 92
reflexiv 98
Reflexivpronomen 98
regelmäßige Verben 6
relative clauses 140
Relativpronomen 140, 142
Relativsatz 140, 146
Richtungsangabe 68
Sammelbegriffe 90
Satzbau 128
sentence structure 128
’s-Genitiv 80, 84
should 58
Signalwörter 26, 32, 46
simple past 6, 26
simple present 20
simple present perfect 32
since 66
so 148
some 88
Subjekt 60
SVOPT 128
there 15
unbestimmter Artikel 102
unregelmäßige Verben 6, 10
Verben der Gefühle 60
Verbform 10
Vergangenheit 26, 36
Verneinung 14, 20, 26, 32, 36, 42, 46
Vokal 21
Vollverb 14
Vorvergangenheit 46
want to 43
was 46
when 16, 46, 150
where 16
who 16
why 16
will 43
will-future 42
zählbare Nomen 86, 90
Zeitangabe 64, 66
Zeitform 14
Zeitpunkt 32, 36
Zeitraum 36
Zeitspanne 32
Zischlaut 21
Zukunft 42
Zustände 21
Zustandsverben 124